# THE LOVE

OF

# JESUS CRUCIFIED

INRI

# The Love

of

# Jesus Crucified

BY

St. ALPHONSUS de LIGUORI,

*Doctor of the Church.*

EDITED BY

REV. EUGENE GRIMM,

*Priest of the Congregation of the Most Holy Redeemer.*

ST. FRANCISVILLE

Cor Jesu Press

2024.

*Published in 2024 by*
**COR JESU PRESS LLC**
www.corjesupress.com

ISBN: 979-8-9891661-8-3

The text of this edition contains selections from *The Complete Works of Saint Alphonsus de Liguori: The Ascetical Works*, Volume IV (*The Passion and Death of Jesus Christ*) and Volume V (*The Mysteries of the Faith*) originally published by Benziger Brothers in 1887.



Cover art and design by P.B. Fossier.

# CONTENTS.

# INVOCATION

OF JESUS AND MARY.

O Saviour of the world, O Love of souls, O Lord most lovely of all beings! Thou by Thy Passion didst come to win to Thyself our hearts, by showing us the immense love that Thou didst bear to us in accomplishing a redemption which has brought to us a sea of benedictions, and which cost Thee a sea of pains and ignominies. It was principally for this end that Thou didst institute the Most Holy Sacrament of the Altar, in order that we might have a perpetual memorial of Thy Passion: "That we might have forever a perpetual memorial of so great a benefit," says St. Thomas, "He gives his body to be the food of the faithful," which St. Paul had already said. *As often as you shall eat this bread, you shall show the death of the Lord.*[1] Oh, how many holy souls hast Thou persuaded by these prodigies of love, consumed by the flames of Thy love, to renounce all earthly goods, in order to dedicate themselves entirely to loving Thee alone, O most amiable Saviour! O my Jesus! I pray Thee make me always remember Thy Passion; and grant that I also, a miserable sinner, overcome at last by so many loving devices, may return to love Thee, and to show Thee, by my poor love, some mark of

[1] 1 *Cor*. xi. 26.

gratitude for the excessive love which Thou, my God and my Saviour, hast borne to me. Remember, my Jesus, that I am one of those sheep of Thine, to save which Thou didst come down on the earth and didst sacrifice Thy divine life. I know that, after having redeemed me by Thy death, Thou hast not ceased to love me, and that Thou dost still bear to me the same love that Thou hadst for me when Thou didst die for my sake. Oh, permit me no longer to lead a life of ingratitude towards Thee, my God, who dost so much deserve to be loved, and hast done so much to be loved by me!

And thou, O most holy Virgin Mary, who didst take so great a part in the Passion of thy Son, obtain for me, I beseech thee, through the merits of thy sorrows, the grace to experience a taste of that compassion which thou didst so sensibly feel at the death of Jesus, and obtain for me also a spark of that love which wrought all the martyrdom of thy afflicted heart. Amen.

"Let my mind, O Lord Jesus Christ, I beseech Thee, be absorbed in the fiery and honeyed sweetness of Thy love, that I may die for love of the love of Thee, who wert pleased to die for love of the love of me." [1]

---

[1] "Absorbeat, quæso, Domine Jesu Christe, mentem meam ignita et melliflua vis amoris tui, ut amore amoris tui moriar, qui amore amoris mei dignatus es mori."— *Prayer of St. Francis Assisi.*

# TO THE READER.

I hope that the little work that I offer you to-day will be pleasing to you, especially since it will put before you, in regular order, the passages of Holy Scripture referring to the love that Jesus Christ showed us in his death; for there is nothing more apt to stimulate a Christian to the love of God than the word of God itself that is drawn from Holy Writ.

Let us, therefore, love Jesus Christ, who is our Saviour, our God, and our supreme good. This is the reason why I invite you to cast a glance at the Passion; for you will find therein all the motives that we can have to hope for eternal life and to love God; and in this our salvation consists.

All the saints cherished a tender devotion towards Jesus Christ in his Passion; this is the only means by which they sanctified themselves. Father Balthasar Alvarez, as we read in his life, used to say that one should not think of having done anything so long as one has not succeeded in constantly keeping in one's heart Jesus crucified. His method of prayer consisted in placing himself at the feet of Jesus crucified, by meditating especially on his poverty, his humiliations, sorrows, and by listening to the lesson that our Lord made him hear from the height of the cross. You may also hope to sanctify yourself if you continue in like manner to consider what your divine Redeemer has done and suffered for you.

Ask him, without ceasing, to give you his love; and this grace you should never weary to ask from your Queen, the Blessed Virgin, who is called the Mother of beautiful love. And when you ask this great gift for yourself, ask it also for me, who have desired to contribute to your sanctification in offering you this little work. I promise to do the same thing for you in order that, one day, in paradise, we may embrace each other as devoted servants of our most amiable Saviour, finding ourselves united there in the society of the elect to see forever, face to face, and love for all eternity, Jesus, our Saviour and our love. Amen.

# INTRODUCTION.

HOW USEFUL IT IS TO MEDITATE ON THE PASSION OF JESUS CHRIST.

The lover of souls, our most loving Redeemer, declared that he had no other motive in coming down upon earth to become man than to enkindle in the hearts of men the fire of his holy love: *I am come to cast fire on earth; and what will I but that it be kindled?* [1] And, oh, what beautiful flames of love has he not enkindled in so many souls, especially by the pains that he chose to suffer in his death, in order to prove to us the immeasurable love which he still bears to us!

Oh, how many souls, happy in the wounds of Jesus, as in burning furnaces of love, have been so inflamed with his love that they have not refused to consecrate to him their goods, their lives, and their whole selves, surmounting with great courage all the difficulties which they had to encounter in the observance of the divine law, for the love of that Lord who, being God, chose to suffer so much for the love of them! This was just the counsel that the Apostle gave us, in order that we might not fail, but make great advances in the way of salvation: *Think diligently upon Him who endureth such opposition from*

[1] *Luke,* xii. 49.

*sinners against Himself, that you be not wearied, fainting in your minds.*[1]

Wherefore St. Augustine, all inflamed with love at the sight of Jesus nailed on the cross, prayed thus sweetly: "Imprint, O Lord, Thy wounds in my heart, that I may read therein suffering and love: suffering, that I may endure for Thee all suffering; love, that I may despise for Thee all love." Write, he said, my most loving Saviour, write on my heart Thy wounds, in order that I may always behold therein Thy sufferings and Thy love. Yes, because, having before my eyes the great sufferings that Thou, my God, didst endure for me, I may bear in silence all the sufferings that it may fall to my lot to endure; and at the sight of the love which Thou didst exhibit for me on the cross, I may never love or be able to love any other than Thee.

And from what source did the saints draw courage and strength to suffer torments, martyrdom, and death, if not from the sufferings of Jesus crucified? St. Joseph of Leonessa, a Capuchin, on seeing that they were going to bind him with cords, for a painful incision that the surgeon was to make in his body, took into his hands his crucifix and said, "Why these cords? why these cords? Behold, these are my chains—my Saviour nailed to the cross for love of me. He, through his sufferings, constrains me to bear every trial for his sake." And thus he suffered the amputation without a complaint; looking upon Jesus,

[1] *Heb.* xii. 3.

who, *as a lamb before his shearers, was dumb, and did not open His mouth.*[1]

Who, then, can ever complain that he suffers wrongfully, when he considers Jesus, who was *bruised for our sins?*[2] Who can refuse to obey, on account of some inconvenience, when Jesus became *obedient unto death?*[3] Who can refuse ignominies, when they behold Jesus treated as a fool, as a mock king, as a disorderly person; struck, spit upon on his face, and suspended upon an infamous gibbet?

Who could love any other object besides Jesus when they see him dying in the midst of so many sufferings and insults, in order to captivate our love? A certain devout solitary prayed to God to teach him what he could do in order to love him perfectly. Our Lord revealed to him that there was no more efficient way to arrive at the perfect love of him than to meditate constantly on his Passion.

For this reason, Father Balthasar Alvarez exhorted his penitents to meditate frequently on the Passion of our Redeemer, telling them that they should not consider that they had done anything at all, until they had arrived at retaining Jesus crucified continually present in their hearts.

"He who desires," says St. Bonaventure, "to go on advancing from virtue to virtue, from grace to grace, should meditate continually on the Passion of Jesus." And he adds that "there is no practice more profitable for the entire sanctification of the soul than the

---

[1] *Isa.* liii. 7.

[2] *Isa.* liii. 5.

[3] *Phil.* ii. 8.

frequent meditation of the sufferings of Jesus Christ."

St. Augustine also said that a single tear shed at the remembrance of the Passion of Jesus is worth more than a pilgrimage to Jerusalem, or a year of fasting on bread and water. Yes, because it was for this end that our Saviour suffered so much, in order that we should think of his sufferings; because if we think on them, it is impossible not to be inflamed with divine love: *The charity of Christ presseth us,*[1] says St. Paul. Jesus is loved by few, because few consider the pains he has suffered for us; but he that frequently considers them cannot live without loving Jesus. "The charity of Christ presseth us." He will feel himself so constrained by his love that he will not find it possible to refrain from loving a God so full of love, who has suffered so much to make us love him.

Therefore the Apostle said that he desired to know nothing but Jesus, and Jesus crucified; that is, the love that he has shown us on the cross: *I judged not myself to know anything among you but Jesus Christ, and Him crucified.*[2] And, in truth, from what books can we better learn the science of the saints—that is, the science of loving God—than from Jesus crucified? That great servant of God, Brother Bernard of Corlione, the Capuchin, not being able to read, his brother religious wanted to teach him, upon which he went to consult his crucifix; but Jesus answered him from the cross, "What is reading? what are books?

---

[1] 2 *Cor.* v. 14.

[2] 1 *Cor.* ii. 2.

Behold, I am the book wherein thou mayst continually read the love I have borne thee." O great subject to be considered during our whole life and during all eternity! A God dead for the love of us! a God dead for the love of us! O wonderful subject!

St. Thomas Aquinas was one day paying a visit to St. Bonaventure, and asked him from what book he had drawn all the beautiful lessons he had written. St. Bonaventure showed him the image of the Crucified, which was completely blackened by all the kisses that he had given it, and said, "This is my book whence I receive everything that I write; and it has taught me whatever little I know."

It was this sweet study of the crucifix which made St. Francis become a great seraph. He wept so continually in meditating on the sufferings of Jesus Christ, that he almost entirely lost his sight. On one occasion, being found crying out and weeping, he was asked what was the matter with him. "What ails me?" answered the saint. "I weep over the sorrows and insults inflicted on my Lord; and my sorrow is increased when I think of those ungrateful men who do not love him, but live without any thought of him." Every time that he heard the bleating of a lamb, he felt himself touched with compassion at the thought of the death of Jesus, the Immaculate Lamb, drained of every drop of blood upon the cross for the sins of the world. And therefore this loving saint could find no subject on which he exhorted his brethren with greater eagerness than the constant remembrance of the Passion of Jesus.

This, then, is the book—Jesus crucified—which, if we constantly read it, will teach us, on the one hand, to have a lively fear of sin, and, on the other hand, will inflame us with love for a God so full of love for us; while we read in these wounds the great malice of sin, which reduced a God to suffer so bitter a death in order to satisfy the divine justice, and the love which our Saviour has shown us in choosing to suffer so much in order to prove to us how much he loved us.

Let us beseech the divine Mother Mary to obtain for us from her Son the grace that we also may enter into these furnaces of love, in which so many loving hearts are consumed, in order that, our earthly affections being there burned away, we also may burn with those blessed flames, which render souls holy on earth and blessed in heaven. Amen.

## REFLECTIONS AND AFFECTIONS

ON THE

# PASSION OF JESUS CHRIST.

---

## CHAPTER I.

### THE LOVE OF JESUS CHRIST IN BEING WILLING TO SATISFY THE DIVINE JUSTICE FOR OUR SINS.

I.

We read in history of a proof of love so prodigious that it will be the admiration of all ages.

There was once a king, lord of many kingdoms, who had one only son, so beautiful, so holy, so amiable, that he was the delight of his father, who loved him as much as himself. This young prince had a great affection for one of his slaves; so much so that, the slave having committed a crime for which he had been condemned to death, the prince offered himself to die for the slave; the father, being jealous of justice, was satisfied to condemn his beloved son to death, in order that the slave might remain free from the punishment that he deserved: and thus the son died a malefactor's death, and the slave was freed from punishment.

This fact, the like of which has never happened in this world, and never will happen, is related in the Gospels, where we read that the Son of God, the Lord of the universe, seeing that man was condemned to eternal death in punishment of his sins, chose to take upon himself human flesh, and thus to pay by his death the penalty due to man: *He was offered because it was His own will.*[1] And his Eternal Father caused him to die upon the cross to save us miserable sinners: *He spared not His own Son, but delivered Him up for us all.*[2] What dost thou think, O devout soul, of this love of the Son and of the Father?

Thou didst, then, O my beloved Redeemer, choose by Thy death to sacrifice Thyself in order to obtain the pardon of my sins. And what return of gratitude shall I then make to Thee? Thou hast done too much to oblige me to love Thee; I should indeed be most ungrateful to Thee if I did not love Thee with my whole heart. Thou hast given for me Thy divine life; I, miserable sinner that I am, give Thee my own life. Yes, I will at least spend that period of life that remains to me only in loving Thee, obeying Thee, and pleasing Thee.

II.

O men, men! let us love this our Redeemer, who, being God, has not disdained to take upon himself our sins, in order to satisfy by his sufferings for the

[1] *Isa.* liii. 7.

[2] *Rom.* viii. 32.

chastisement which we have deserved: *Surely He hath borne our infirmities, and carried our sorrows.*[1]

St. Augustine says that our Lord in creating us formed us by virtue of his power, but in redeeming us he has saved us from death by means of his sufferings: "He created us in his strength; he sought us back in his weakness."

How much do I not owe Thee, O Jesus my Saviour! Oh, if I were to give my blood a thousand times over,—if I were to spend a thousand lives for Thee,—it would yet be nothing. Oh, how could any one that meditated much on the love which Thou hast shown him in Thy Passion, love anything else but Thee? Through the love with which Thou didst love us on the cross, grant me the grace to love Thee with my whole heart. I love Thee, infinite Goodness; I love Thee above every other good; and I ask nothing more of Thee but Thy holy love.

"But how is this?" continues St. Augustine. How is it possible, O Saviour of the world, that Thy love has arrived at such a height that when I had committed the crime, Thou shouldst have to pay the penalty? "Whither has Thy love reached? I have sinned; Thou art punished."

And what could it then signify to Thee, adds St. Bernard, that we should lose ourselves and be chastised, as we well deserved to be; that Thou shouldst choose to satisfy with Thy innocent flesh for our sins, and to die in order to deliver us from death! "O good Jesus, what doest Thou? We ought to have died, and

[1] *Isa.* liii. 4.

it is Thou who dies. We have sinned and Thou sufferest. A deed without precedent, grace without merit, charity without measure." O deed which never has had and never will have its match! O grace which we could never merit! O love which can never be understood!

III.

*Christ hath redeemed us from the curse of the law, being made a curse for us (for it is written, Cursed is every one that hangeth on a tree): that the blessing of Abraham might come to the Gentiles through Jesus Christ.*[1] "He was made a curse upon the cross," says St. Ambrose, "that thou mightest be blessed in the kingdom of God."

O my dearest Saviour! Thou wert, then, content, in order to obtain for me the blessing of God, to embrace the dishonor of appearing upon the cross accursed in the sight of the whole world, and even forsaken in Thy sufferings by Thy Eternal Father,—a suffering which made Thee cry out with a loud voice, *My God, My God, why hast Thou forsaken Me?*[2] Yes, observes Simon of Cassia, it was for this end that Jesus was abandoned in his Passion in order that we might not remain abandoned in the sins which we have committed: "Therefore Christ was abandoned in his sufferings that we might not be abandoned in our guilt." O prodigy of compassion! O excess of love of God towards men! And how can

[1] *Gal.* iii. 13.

[2] *Matt.* xxvii. 46.

there be a soul who believes this, O my Jesus, and yet loves Thee not?

IV.

*He hath loved us, and washed us from our sins in His own blood.*[1] Behold, O men, how far the love of Jesus for us has carried him, in order to cleanse us from the filthiness of our sins. He has even shed every drop of his blood that he might prepare for us in this his own blood a bath of salvation.

Whereupon St. Bonaventure exclaims, "O good Jesus, what hast Thou done?" O my Saviour, what indeed hast Thou done? How far hath Thy love carried Thee? What hast Thou seen in me which hath made Thee love me so much? "Wherefore hast Thou loved me so much? Why, Lord, why? What am I?" Wherefore didst Thou choose to suffer so much for me? Who am I that Thou wouldst win to Thyself my love at so dear a price? Oh, it was entirely the work of Thy infinite love! Be Thou eternally praised and blessed for it.

*O all ye that pass by the way, attend and see if there be any sorrow like to My sorrow.*[2] The same seraphic Doctor, considering these words of Jeremias as spoken of our blessed Redeemer while he was hanging on the cross dying for the love of us, says, "Yes, Lord, I will attend and see if there be any love like unto Thy love." By which he means, I do indeed see and understand, O my most loving Redeemer, how much Thou didst suffer upon that infamous tree;

---

[1] *Apoc.* i. 5.
[2] *Lam.* i. 12.

but what most constrains me to love Thee is the thought of the affection which Thou hast shown me in suffering so much, in order that I might love Thee.

V.

That which most inflamed St. Paul with the love of Jesus was the thought that he chose to die, not only for all men, but for him in particular: *He loved me, and delivered Himself up for me.*[1] Yes, he has loved me, said he, and for my sake he gave himself up to die. And thus ought every one of us to say; for St. John Chrysostom asserts that God has loved every individual man with the same love with which he has loved the world: "He loves each man separately with the same measure of charity with which he loves the whole world." So that each one of us is under as great obligation to Jesus Christ for having suffered for every one, as if he had suffered for him alone.

For supposing, my brother, Jesus Christ had died to save you alone, leaving all others to their original ruin, what a debt of gratitude you would owe to him! But you ought to feel that you owe him a greater obligation still for having died for the salvation of all. For if he had died for you alone, what sorrow would it not have caused you to think that your neighbors, parents, brothers, and friends would be damned, and that you would, when this life was over, be forever separated from them? If you and your family had been slaves, and some one came to rescue you alone, how would you not entreat of him to save your

---

[1] *Gal.* ii. 20.

parents and brothers together with yourself! And how much would you thank him if he did this to please you! Say, therefore, to Jesus:

O my sweetest Redeemer! Thou hast done this for me without my having asked Thee; Thou hast not only saved me from death at the price of Thy blood, but also my parents and friends, so that I may have a good hope that we may all together enjoy Thy presence forever in paradise. O Lord! I thank Thee, and I love Thee, and I hope to thank Thee for it, and to love Thee forever in that blessed country.

VI.

Who could ever, says St. Laurence Justinian, explain the love which the divine Word bears to each one of us, since it surpasses the love of every son towards his mother, and of every mother for her son? "The intense charity of the Word of God surpasses all maternal and filial love; neither can human words express how great his love is to each one of us!" So much so, that our Lord revealed to St. Gertrude that he would be ready to die as many times as there were souls damned, if they were yet capable of redemption: "I would die as many deaths as there are souls in hell."

O Jesus, O treasure more worthy of love than all others! why is it that men love Thee so little? Oh! do Thou make known what Thou hast suffered for each of them, the love that Thou bearest them, the desire Thou hast to be loved by them, and how worthy Thou art of being loved. Make Thyself known, O my Jesus, make Thyself loved.

VII.

*I am the good shepherd,* said our Redeemer; *the good shepherd gives his life for his sheep.*[1] But, O my Lord, where are there in the world shepherds like unto Thee? Other shepherds will slay their sheep in order to preserve their own life. Thou, O too loving Shepherd, didst give Thy divine life in order to save the life of Thy beloved sheep. And of these sheep, I, O most amiable Shepherd, have the happiness to be one. What obligation, then, am I not under to love Thee, and to spend my life for Thee, since Thou hast died for the love of me in particular! And what confidence ought I not to have in Thy blood, knowing that it has been shed to pay the debt of my sins! *And thou shalt say in that day, I will give thanks to Thee, O Lord. Behold, God is my Saviour; I will deal confidently, and will not fear.*[2] And how can I any longer mistrust Thy mercy, O my Lord, when I behold Thy wounds? Come, then, O sinners, and let us have recourse to Jesus, who hangs upon that cross as it were upon a throne of mercy. He has appeased the divine justice, which we had insulted. If we have offended God, he has done penance for us; all that is required for us is contrition for our sins. O my dearest Saviour, to what have Thy pity and love for me reduced Thee? The slave sins, and Thou, Lord, payest the penalty for him. If, therefore, I think of my sins, the thought of the punishment I deserve must make me tremble; but when I think of Thy death, I find I have more

---

[1] *John*, x. 11.

[2] *Isa.* xii. 1.

reason to hope than to fear. O blood of Jesus! thou art all my hope.

VIII.

But this blood, as it inspires us with confidence, also obliges us to give ourselves entirely to our Blessed Redeemer. The Apostle exclaims, *Know you not that you are not your own? For you are bought with a great price.*[1]

Therefore, O my Jesus, I cannot any longer, without injustice, dispose of myself, or of my own concerns, since Thou hast made me Thine by purchasing me through Thy death. My body, my soul, my life are no longer mine; they are Thine, and entirely Thine. In Thee alone, therefore, will I hope. O my God, crucified and dead for me, I have nothing else to offer Thee but this soul, which Thou hast bought with Thy blood; to Thee do I offer it. Accept of my love, for I desire nothing but Thee, my Saviour, my God, my love, my all. Hitherto I have shown much gratitude towards men; to Thee alone have I, alas! been most ungrateful. But now I love Thee, and I have no greater cause of sorrow than my having offended Thee. O my Jesus, give me confidence in Thy Passion; root out of my heart every affection that belongs not to Thee. I will love Thee alone, who dost deserve all my love, and who hast given me so much reason to love Thee. O Mary, O Mother of fair love, I pray thee, through the merits of thy burning heart, obtain for me the grace to live only in order to love thy Son, who, being in himself worthy of an infinite

---

[1] 1 *Cor.* vi. 19.

love, has chosen at so great a cost to acquire to himself the love of a miserable sinner like me. O love of souls, O my Jesus! I love Thee, I love Thee, I love Thee; but still I love Thee too little. Oh, give me more love, give me flames that may make me live always burning with Thy love! I do not myself deserve it; but Thou dost well deserve it, O infinite Goodness. Amen. This I hope, so may it be.

# CHAPTER II.

## JESUS CHOSE TO SUFFER SO MUCH FOR US, IN ORDER THAT WE MAY UNDERSTAND THE GREAT LOVE HE HAS FOR US.

### I.

Jesus Christ could easily have obtained for us salvation without suffering, and in leading a life of ease and delight; but no, St. Paul says, *having joy set before Him, He endured the cross.*[1] He refused the riches, the delights, the honors of the world, and chose for himself a life of poverty, and a death full of suffering and ignominy. And wherefore? Would it not have sufficed for him to have offered to his eternal Father one single prayer for the pardon of man? for this prayer, being of infinite value, would have been sufficient to save the world, and infinite worlds besides. Why, then, did he choose for himself so much suffering, and a death so cruel, that an author has said very truly, that through mere pain the soul of Jesus separated itself from his body? To what purpose so much cost in order to save man? St. John Chrysostom answers, a single prayer of Jesus would indeed have sufficed to redeem us; but it was not sufficient to show us the love that our God has borne us: "That which sufficed to redeem us was not sufficient for love." And St. Thomas confirms this when he says, "Christ, in suffering from love, offered to God more than the expiation of the offence of the human

[1] *Heb.* xii. 2.

race demanded." Because Jesus loved us so much, he desired to be loved very much by us; and therefore he did everything that he could, even unto suffering for us, in order to conciliate our love, and to show that there was nothing more that he could do to make us love him: "He endured much weariness," says St. Bernard, "that he might bind man to love him much."

II.

And what greater proof of love, says our Saviour himself, can a friend show towards the person he loves than to give his life for his sake? *Greater love than this no man hath, that a man lay down his life for his friends.*[1] But Thou, O most loving Jesus, says St. Bernard, hast done more than this, since Thou hast given Thy life for us, who were not Thy friends, but Thy enemies, and rebels against Thee: "Thou hast a greater charity, Lord, in giving Thy life for Thy enemies." And this is what the Apostle observes when he writes, *He commendeth His charity towards us, because when as yet we were sinners, according to the time Christ died for us.*[2]

Thou wouldst then die for me, Thy enemy, O my Jesus; and yet can I resist so much love? Behold, here I am; since Thou dost so anxiously desire that I should love Thee, I will drive away every other love from my breast, and will love Thee alone.

---

[1] *John*, xv. 13.

[2] *Rom.* v. 8.

III.

St. John Chrysostom says that the principal end Jesus had in his Passion was to discover to us his love, and thus to draw our hearts to himself by the remembrance of the pains that he has endured for us: "This was the principal cause of the Passion of our Lord; he wished it to be known how great was the love of God for man,—of God, who would rather be loved than feared." St. Thomas adds that we may, through the Passion of Jesus, know the greatness of the love that God bears to man: "By this man understands the greatness of the love of God to man." And St. John had said before, *In this we have known the charity of God, because He hath laid down his life for us.*[1]

IV.

St. Luke relates that Moses and Elias on Mount Tabor, speaking of the Passion of Jesus Christ, called it an excess: *And they spoke of his excess that he should accomplish in Jerusalem.*[2] "Yes," says St. Bonaventure, and rightly was the Passion of Jesus called an excess; for "it was an excess of suffering and an excess of love." And a devout author adds, "What more could he suffer that he has not endured? The excess of his love reached the highest point." Yes, indeed; for the divine law imposes on men no other

---

[1] 1 *John*, iii. 16.

[2] *Luke*, ix. 31.

obligation than that of loving their neighbors as themselves; but Jesus has loved man more than himself: "He loved these more than himself," says St. Cyril.

Thou didst, then, O my beloved Redeemer,—I will say to Thee with St. Augustine,—love me more than Thyself, since to save me Thou wouldst lose Thy divine life,—a life infinitely more precious than the lives of all men and angels put together. Thou didst love me more than Thyself, because Thou wert willing to die for me.

V.

It is a pleasing thing to see a person beloved by some great man, and more so if the latter has the power of raising him to some great fortune; but how much more sweet and pleasing must it be to us to see ourselves beloved by God, who can raise us up to an eternity of happiness? Under the old law men might have doubted whether God loved them with a tender love; but after having seen him shed his blood on an infamous gibbet and die for us, how can we doubt his loving us with infinite tenderness and affection? O my soul, behold now thy Jesus, hanging from the cross all covered with wounds! behold how, by these wounds, he proves to thee the love of his enamoured heart: "The secrets of his heart are revealed through the wounds of his body," says St. Bernard.

My dearest Jesus, I am greatly consoled and inflamed with love for Thee, when I see by means of these wounds the love that Thou bearest me. O heavenly seraphs, what do you think of the love of my God, *who loved me and delivered Himself for me*?[1]

VI.

St. Paul says that when the Gentiles heard it preached that Jesus was crucified for the love of men, they thought it such nonsense that they could not believe it. *But we preach Christ crucified, unto the Jews, indeed, a stumbling-block, and unto the Gentiles foolishness.*[2] And how is it possible, said they, to believe that an omnipotent God, who wants nothing in order to be perfectly happy as he is, would choose to become man and die on a cross to save men? This would be the same, said they, as to believe that a God had become mad for love of men: *But unto the Gentiles foolishness.* And thus they refused to believe it. But faith teaches us that Jesus has really undertaken and accomplished this great work of redemption which the Gentiles esteemed and called folly. "We have seen," says St. Laurence Justinian, "Eternal Wisdom, the only-begotten of God, become as it were a fool through the excessive love he bears man." Yes, adds Cardinal Hugo, for: "It seemed a folly that God should die for the salvation of men."

The Blessed Giacopone, who in this world had been a man of letters, and afterwards became a Franciscan, seemed to have become mad through the love that he bore to Jesus Christ. One day Jesus appeared to him and said, Giacopone, why do you commit these

[1] *Gal.* ii. 20.

[2] 1 *Cor.* i. 23.

follies? "Why," he answered, "because Thou hast taught them me. If I am mad," said he; "Thou hast been more mad than I, in that Thou hast died for me. I am a fool, for Thou hast been a greater fool."

Thus, also, St. Mary Magdalen of Pazzi, being in an ecstasy, exclaimed, "O God of love! O God of love! The love that Thou bearest to creatures, O my Jesus, is too great indeed." And one day, when quite enraptured, she took an image of the Crucified, and began running about the monastery, crying, "O Love! Love! I shall never rest, my God, from calling Thee Love." Then turning to the religious, she said, "Do you not know, my dear sisters, that Jesus Christ is nothing but love? He is even mad with love, and I will go on saying it continually." And she added that she wished she could be heard by the whole universe when she called Jesus "Love," in order that the love of Jesus might be known and loved by all. And she sometimes even began to ring the bell, in order that all the people in the world should come (as she desired, if it had been possible) to love her Jesus.

Yes, my sweetest Redeemer, permit me to say so, this Thy spouse was indeed right when she called Thee mad with love. And does it not indeed seem a folly that Thou shouldst choose to die for love of me, for so ungrateful a worm as I am, and whose offences Thou didst foresee, as well as the infidelities of which I should be guilty? But if Thou, my God, art thus become mad, as it were, for the love of me, how is it that I do not become mad for the love of a God? When I have seen Thee crucified and dead for me, how is it that I can think of any other than Thee? I promise for the future to love none other but Thee, and to think constantly on the love Thou hast shown me by dying in the midst of so many sufferings for me. O scourges, O thorns, O nails, O cross, O wounds, O sufferings, O death of my Saviour! you irresistibly constrain me to love him who has so much loved me. I would fain love Thee so much that I should find no pleasure but in pleasing Thee, my most sweet Lord; and since Thou dost so earnestly desire my love, I protest that I will only live for Thee. I desire to do whatever Thou wiliest of me. O my Jesus! I pray Thee, help me, and grant that I may please Thee entirely and continually in time and in eternity. Mary, my Mother, entreat Jesus for me, in order that he may grant me his holy love; for I desire nothing else in this world and in the next but to love Jesus. Amen.

# CHAPTER III.

## JESUS, FOR LOVE OF US, CHOSE TO SUFFER THE PAINS OF HIS PASSION, EVEN FROM THE BEGINNING OF HIS LIFE.

I.

The divine Word came into the world and took upon him human flesh in order to make himself loved of man, and therefore he came with such a longing to suffer for our sake, that he would not lose a moment in beginning to torment himself, at least by apprehension. Hardly was he conceived in the womb of Mary, when he represented to his mind all the sufferings of his Passion; and, in order to obtain for us pardon and divine grace, he offered himself to his eternal Father to satisfy for us through his dolors all the chastisements due to our sins; and from that moment he began to suffer everything that he afterwards endured in his most bitter death.

O my most loving Redeemer! what have I hitherto done or suffered for Thee? If I could for a thousand years endure for Thy sake all the torments that all the martyrs have suffered, they would yet be nothing compared with that one first moment in which Thou didst offer Thyself and begin to suffer for me.

II.

The martyrs did indeed suffer great pains and ignominy; but they only endured them at the time of their martyrdom. Jesus even from the first instant of his life continually suffered all the torments of his Passion; for, from the first moment, he had before his eyes all the horrid scene of torments and insults which he was to receive from men. Wherefore he said by the mouth of the prophet, *My sorrow is continually before me.*[1] O my Jesus! Thou hast been so desirous to suffer for my sake that Thou wouldst even endure Thy sufferings before the time; and yet I am so desirous after the pleasures of this world. How many times have I offended Thee in order to please my body! O my Lord! through the merits of Thy sufferings, take away from me, I beseech Thee, all affection for earthly pleasures. For Thy love I desire to abstain from this satisfaction. [*Mention it.*]

III.

God, in his compassion for us, does not generally reveal to us the trials that await us before the time when we are destined to endure them. If a criminal who is executed on a gibbet had had revealed to him from the first use of his reason the torture that awaited him, could he even have been capable of joy?

Our kind Redeemer, even from the first instant of his life, had always present before him the scourges, the thorns, the cross, the outrages of his Passion, the desolate death that awaited him. When he beheld the victims which were sacrificed in the temple, he well knew that they were figures of the sacrifice which he, the Immaculate Lamb, would one day consummate on the altar of the cross. When he saw his dear Mother, he already imagined that he saw her in an

---

[1] *Ps.* xxxvii. 18.

agony of suffering at the foot of the cross, near his dying self.

So that, O my Jesus, the horrible sight of all these evils kept Thee during the whole of Thy life continually tormented and afflicted before the time of Thy death. And Thou didst accept and suffer everything for my sake. O my agonizing Lord! the sight alone of all the sins of the world, especially of mine, by which Thou didst already foresee I should offend Thee, rendered Thy life more afflicted and painful than all the lives that ever have been or ever will be. O my Lord, make me know the greatness of Thy love, in order that I may no longer be ungrateful to Thee. Oh, if I but loved Thee, my Jesus,—if I really loved Thee,—how sweet it would be to me to suffer for Thee!

IV.

Jesus appeared one day on the cross to Sister Magdalen Orsini, who had been suffering for some time from some great affliction, and animated her to suffer it in peace. The servant of God answered, "But, Lord, Thou didst only hang on the cross for three hours, whereas I have gone on suffering this pain for several years." Jesus Christ then said to her reproachingly, "O ignorant that thou art, what dost thou mean? From the first moment that I was in my Mother's womb, I suffered in my heart all that I afterwards endured on the cross."

And I, my dear Redeemer, how can I, at the sight of such great sufferings which Thou didst endure for my sake, during Thy whole life, complain of those crosses which Thou dost send me for my good. I have hitherto done nothing for Thee. My Jesus, help me to suffer something for Thy love before death overtakes me. I am ashamed of appearing before Thee; but I will no longer be ungrateful, as I have been so many years towards Thee. Thou hast deprived Thyself of every pleasure for me; I will for the love of Thee renounce all the pleasures of the senses. Thou hast suffered so many pains for me; I will for Thy sake suffer all the pains of my life and of my death as it shall best please Thee. Thou hast been forsaken; I will be content that all should forsake me, provided Thou dost not forsake me, O my only and sovereign good! Thou hast been persecuted; I accept whatever persecution may befall me. Finally, Thou hast died for me; I will die for Thee. O my Jesus, my Treasure, my love, my all! I love Thee. Oh, give me more love! Amen.

# CHAPTER IV.

## THE GREAT DESIRE WHICH JESUS HAD TO SUFFER AND TO DIE FOR LOVE OF US.

I.

Oh, how exceedingly tender, loving, and constraining was that declaration of our Blessed Redeemer concerning his coming into the world, when he said that he had come to kindle in souls the fire of divine love, and that his only desire was that this holy flame should be enkindled in the hearts of men: *I am come to cast fire upon the earth; and what will I but that it should be kindled?* [1] He continued immediately to say that he was expecting to be baptized with the baptism of his own blood—not, indeed, to wash out his own sins, since he was incapable of sinning, but to wash out our sins, which he had come to satisfy by his sufferings: "The Passion of Christ is called baptism, because we are purified in his blood." And therefore our loving Jesus, in order to make us understand how ardent was his desire to die for us, added, with sweetest expression of his love, that he felt an immense longing for the time of his Passion, so great was his desire to suffer for our sake. These are his loving words: *I have a baptism wherewith I am to be baptized; and how am I straitened until it be accomplished?* [2]

---

[1] *Luke*, xii. 49.

[2] *Luke*, xii. 50.

O God. the lover of men, what more couldst Thou have said or done in order to put me under the necessity of loving Thee? And what good could my love ever do Thee, that Thou didst choose to die, and didst so much desire death in order to obtain it? If a servant of mine had only desired to die for me, he would have attracted my love; and can I then live without loving Thee with all my heart, my king and God, who didst die for me, and who hadst such a longing for death in order to acquire to Thyself my love?

II.

But behold our loving Jesus already on the point of being sacrificed on the Altar of the Cross for our salvation, in that blessed night which preceded his Passion. Let us hear him saying to his disciples, in the last supper that he makes with them, *With desire have I desired to eat this pasch with you.*[1] St. Laurence Justinian, considering these words, asserts that they were all words of love: "With desire have I desired; this is the voice of love." As if our loving Redeemer had said, O men, know that this night, in which my Passion will begin, has been the time most longed after by me during the whole of my life; because I shall now make known to you, through my sufferings and my bitter death, how much I love you, and shall thereby oblige you to love me in the strongest way it is possible for me to do.

O sovereign God! Thou hast given Thyself entirely to me; and how, then, shall I not love Thee with my whole self? I believe,—yes, I believe Thou hast died

[1] *Luke*, xxii. 15.

for me; and how can I, then, love Thee so little as constantly to forget Thee, and all that Thou hast suffered for me? And why, Lord, when I think on Thy Passion, am I not quite inflamed with Thy love, and do I not become entirely Thine, like so many holy souls who, after meditating on Thy sufferings, have remained the happy prey of Thy love, and have given themselves entirely to Thee?

III.

The spouse in the Canticles said that whenever her Spouse introduced her into the sacred cellar of his Passion, she saw herself so assaulted on all sides by divine love that, all languishing with love, she was constrained to seek for relief to her wounded heart: *The king brought me into the cellar of wine, he set in order charity in me. Stay me up with flowers, compass me about with apples; because I languish with love.*[1] And how is it possible for a soul to enter upon the meditation of the Passion of Jesus Christ without being wounded, as by so many darts of love, by those sufferings and agonies which so greatly afflicted the body and soul of our loving Lord, and without being sweetly constrained to love him who loved her so much?

O Immaculate Lamb, thus lacerated, covered with blood, and disfigured, as I behold Thee on this cross, how beautiful and how worthy of love dost Thou yet appear to me! Yes, because all these wounds that I behold in Thee are to me signs and proofs of the great love that Thou bearest to me. Oh, if all men did but

---

[1] *Cant.* ii. 4.

contemplate Thee often in that state in which Thou wert one day made a spectacle to all Jerusalem, who could help being seized with Thy love? O my beloved Lord, accept me to love Thee, since I give Thee all my senses and all my will. And how can I refuse Thee anything, if Thou hast not refused me Thy blood, Thy life, and all Thyself?

IV.

St. Laurence Justinian, in considering this word "I thirst," which Jesus pronounced on the cross when he was expiring, says that this thirst was not a thirst which proceeded from dryness, but one that arose from the ardor of the love that Jesus had for us: "This thirst springs from the fever of his love." Because by this word our Redeemer intended to declare to us, more than the thirst of the body, the desire that he had of suffering for us, by showing us his love: and the immense desire that he had of being loved by us, by the many sufferings that he endured for us: "This thirst proceeds from the fever of his love."

O God, enamoured of souls, is it possible that such an excess of goodness can remain without correspondence on our part? It is said that love must be repaid by love; but by what love can Thy love ever be repaid? It would be necessary for another God to die for Thee, in order to compensate for the love that Thou hast borne us in dying for us. And how, then, couldst Thou, O my Lord, say that Thy delight was to dwell with men, if Thou dost receive from them nothing but injuries and ill-treatment? Love made Thee, then, change into delights the sufferings and the insults that Thou hast endured for us. O my Redeemer, most worthy of love, I will no longer resist the stratagems of Thy love; I give Thee from henceforth my whole love. Thou art and shalt be always the only beloved one of my soul. O my Jesus! assist, I pray Thee, by Thy merits, this desire which Thou dost Thyself give me. O infinite God, I believe in Thee, I hope m Thee, I love Thee. Mary, my Mother, intercede for me. Amen.

# CHAPTER V.

## THE LOVE OF JESUS IN LEAVING HIMSELF FOR OUR FOOD BEFORE HIS DEATH.

### I.

*Jesus, knowing that His hour was come that He should pass out of this world to the Father, having loved His own who were in the world, He loved them to the end.*[1] Our most loving Redeemer, on the last night of his life, knowing that the much-longed-for time had arrived on which he should die for the love of man, had not the heart to leave us alone in this valley of tears; but in order that he might not be separated from us even by death, he would leave us his whole self as food in the Sacrament of the Altar; giving us to understand by this that, having given us this gift of infinite worth, he could give us nothing further to prove to us his love: *He loved them unto the end.* Cornelius à Lapide, with St. Chrysostom and Theophylact, interprets the words "unto the end" according to the Greek text, and writes thus: "He loved them with an excessive and supreme love." Jesus in this sacrament made his last effort of love towards men, as the Abbot Guerric says: "He poured out the whole power of his love upon his friends."

This was still better expressed by the holy Council of Trent, which, in speaking of the Sacrament of the Altar, says that our Blessed Saviour "poured out of

[1] *John*, xiii. 1.

himself in it, as it were, all the riches of his love towards us."

St. Mary Magdalen of Pazzi said that a soul, after having communicated, might say, "It is consummated;" that is to say, My God, having given himself to me in this Holy Communion, has nothing more to give me. This saint, one day asked one of her novices what she had been thinking of after Communion; she answered, "Of the *love of Jesus.*" "Yes," replied the saint; "when we think of this love, we cannot pass on to other thoughts, but must stop upon love."

O Saviour of the world, what dost Thou expect from men, that Thou hast been induced even to give them Thyself in food? And what can there be left to Thee to give us after this Sacrament, in order to oblige us to love Thee? Ah, my most loving God, enlighten me that I may know what an excess of goodness this has been of Thine, to reduce Thyself unto becoming my food in Holy Communion! If Thou hast, therefore, given Thyself entirely to me, it is just that I also should give myself wholly to Thee. Come, therefore, and come often, into my soul, and make it entirely Thine. Oh that I could truly say to Thee, as the loving St. Philip Neri said to Thee when he received Thee in the Viaticum, "Behold my love, behold my love; give me my love."

II.

*He that eateth My flesh, and drinketh My blood, abideth in Me, and I in him.*[1] St. Denis, the Areopagite, says that love always tends towards union with

---

[1] *John*, vi. 57.

the object beloved. And because food becomes one thing with him who eats it, therefore our Lord would reduce himself to food, in order that, receiving him in Holy Communion, we might become of one substance with him: *Take ye and eat,* said Jesus; *this is My body*. As if he had said, remarks St. John Chrysostom, "Eat Me, that the highest union may take place." O man, feed thyself on Me, in order that thou and I may become one substance. In the same way, says St. Cyril of Alexandria, as two pieces of melted wax unite together, so a soul that communicates is so thoroughly united to Jesus that Jesus remains in it, and it in Jesus.

O infinite love, worthy of infinite love, when shall I love Thee, my Jesus, as Thou hast loved me? O divine food, Sacrament of love, when wilt Thou draw me entirely to Thyself? Thou hast nothing left to do in order to make Thyself loved by me. I am constantly intending to begin to love Thee, I constantly promise Thee to do so; but I never begin. I will from this day begin to love Thee in earnest. Oh, do Thou enable me to do so. Enlighten me, inflame me, detach me from earth, and permit me not any longer to resist so many enticements of Thy love.

III.

St. Paul remarks also on the time which Jesus chooses to make us this gift of the most Holy Sacrament. The Apostle remarks that *The Lord Jesus, the same night in which He was betrayed, took bread, and, giving thanks, broke and said, Take ye and eat;*

*this is my body which shall be delivered for you.*[1] In that same night, then, when men were thinking of preparing torments and death for Jesus, our beloved Redeemer thought of leaving them himself in the Blessed Sacrament; giving us thereby to understand that his love was so great that, instead of being cooled by so many injuries, it was then more than ever yearning towards us. O most loving Saviour, how couldst Thou have so great love for men as to choose to remain with them on this earth to be their food, after they had driven Thee away from it with so much ingratitude!

Let us also remark the immense desire which Jesus had during all his life for the arrival of that night in which he had determined to leave us this great pledge of his love. For at the moment of his instituting this most sweet sacrament he said, *With desire I have desired to eat this pasch with you;*[2] words which discover to us the ardent desire which he had to unite himself to us in Communion through the love which he bore us: "This is the voice of most burning charity," says St. Laurence Justinian. And Jesus still retains at the present time the same desire towards all the souls that love him. There is not a bee, said he one day to St. Matilda, that throws itself with such eagerness upon the flowers in order to suck out the honey, as I, through the violence of my love, hasten to the soul that desires me.

---

[1] 1 *Cor.* xi. 23.

[2] *Luke,* xxii. 15.

O lover, too full of love, there are no greater proofs left for Thee to give me in order to persuade me that Thou dost love me. I bless Thy goodness for it. O my Jesus, I beseech Thee, draw me entirely to Thyself. Make me love Thee henceforth with all the affections and tenderness of which I am capable. Oh, help me to love Thee; I ask nothing more of Thee.

IV.

St. Bernard says that God loves us for no other reason than that he may be loved by us: "God only loved that he might be loved." And therefore our Saviour protested that he had come upon earth in order to make himself loved: *I am come to send a fire upon the earth.*[1] And oh, what flames of holy love does Jesus kindle in souls in this most divine Sacrament! The Venerable Father Francis Olimpio, a Theatine, said that nothing was so fit to excite our hearts to love the sovereign good as the most Holy Communion. Hesychius called Jesus in the Sacrament a "divine fire." And St. Catharine of Sienna, one day perceiving, in the hands of a priest, Jesus in the Sacrament under the appearance of a furnace of love, was full of astonishment that the whole world was not consumed by the fire. The Abbot Rupert, and St. Gregory of Nyssa said that the altar itself was the wine-cellar where the espoused soul is inebriated with the love of her Lord; so much so, that, forgetful of earth, it burns and languishes with holy love: *The king brought me,* says the spouse in the Canticles, *into the cellar of wine; he set in order charity in me.*

[1] *Luke,* xii. 49.

*Stay me up with flowers, compass me about with apples; because I languish with love.*[1]

O love of my soul, most Holy Sacrament; oh that I could always remember Thee, to forget everything else, and that I could love Thee alone without interruption and without reserve! Ah, my Jesus, Thou hast knocked so frequently at the door of my heart, that Thou hast at last, I hope, entered therein. But since Thou hast entered there, drive away, I pray Thee, all its affections that do not tend towards Thyself. Possess Thyself so entirely of me, that I may be able with truth to say to Thee from this day forth, with the Prophet, *What have I in heaven? and besides Thee what do I desire on earth? The God of my heart, and my portion forever.*[2] Yes, O my God, what else do I desire but Thee upon earth or in heaven? Thou alone art and shalt always be the only Lord of my heart and my will; and Thou alone shalt be all my portion, all my riches, in this life and in the next.

V.

Go, said the Prophet Isaias—go, publish everywhere the loving inventions of our God, in order to make himself loved of men: *You shall draw waters with joy out of the Saviour's fountains; and you shall say in that day, Praise ye the Lord, and call upon His name, make His inventions known among the people.*[3] And what inventions has not the love of Jesus made in order to make himself loved by us? Even on the

---

[1] *Cant.* ii. 4.

[2] *Ps.* lxxii. 25.

[3] *Isa.* xii. 3.

cross he has opened in his wounds so many fountains of grace, that to receive them it is sufficient to ask for them in faith. And, not satisfied with this, he has given us his whole self in the Most Holy Sacrament.

O man, says St. John Chrysostom, wherefore art thou so niggardly, and dost use so much reserve in thy love for that God who hath given his whole self to thee without any reserve? "He gave himself wholly to thee, reserving nothing for himself." Behold, adds St. Bonaventure, that immense God, "whom the world cannot contain, become our prisoner and captive" when we receive him into our breast in Holy Communion. Wherefore St. Bernard, transported with love when he considered this, exclaimed, My Jesus would make himself "the inseparable guest of my heart." And since my God, he concludes, has chosen to "spend himself entirely for my sake," it is reasonable that I should employ all that I am in serving and loving him.

Ah, my beloved Jesus, tell me, what more is there left for Thee to invent in order to make Thyself loved? And shall I, then, continue to live so ungrateful to Thee as I have hitherto done? My Lord, permit it not. I bless Thee that Thou dost give me time to weep over the offences that I have committed against Thee, and to love Thee in this world. During the life that remains to me, I will place all my affections in Thee, and endeavor to please Thee as much as I possibly can. Help me, O my Jesus; forsake me not, I beseech Thee. Save me by Thy merits, and let my salvation be to love Thee always in this life and in eternity. Mary, my Mother, do thou also assist me.

# CHAPTER VI.

## THE BLOODY SWEAT AND AGONY SUFFERED BY JESUS IN THE GARDEN.

### I.

Behold, our most loving Saviour, having come to the Garden of Gethsemani, did of his own accord make a beginning of his bitter Passion by giving full liberty to the passions of fear, of weariness, and of sorrow to come and afflict him with all their torments: *He began to fear; and to be heavy,*[1] *to grow sorrowful, and to be sad.*[2]

He began, then, first to feel a great fear of death, and of the sufferings he would have soon to endure. *He began to fear*; but how? Was it not he who had so much desired this hour of his Passion, and who had said shortly before, *With desire have I desired to eat this Pasch with you?*[3] And yet how is it that he was seized with such a fear of death, that he even prayed his Father to deliver him from it? *My Father, if it be possible, let this chalice pass from Me.*[4] The Venerable Bede answers this, and says, "He prays that the chalice may pass from him, in order to show that he was truly man." He, our loving Saviour, chose indeed to die for us in order by his death to prove to us the

---

[1] *Mark*, xiv. 33.
[2] *Matt.* xxvi. 37.
[3] *Luke*, xxii. 15.
[4] *Matt.* xxvi. 39.

love that he bore us; but in order that men might not suppose that he had assumed a fantastic body (as some heretics have blasphemously asserted), or that by virtue of his divinity he had died without suffering any pain, He therefore made this prayer to his heavenly Father, not indeed with a view of being heard, but to give us to understand that he died as man, and afflicted with a great fear of death and of the sufferings which should accompany his death.

O most amiable Jesus! Thou wouldst, then, take upon Thee our fearfulness in order to give us Thy courage in suffering the trials of this life. Oh, be Thou forever blessed for Thy great mercy and love! Oh, may all our hearts love Thee as much as Thou desirest, and as much as Thou deservest!

II.

*He began to be heavy.* He began to feel a great weariness on account of the torments that were prepared for Him. When one is weary, even pleasures are painful. Oh, what anguish united to this weariness must Jesus Christ have felt at the horrible representation which then came before his mind, of all the torments, both exterior and interior, which, during the short remainder of his life, were so cruelly to afflict his body and his blessed soul! Then did all the sufferings he was to endure pass distinctly before his eyes, as well as all the insults that he should endure from the Jews and from the Romans; and, above all, he had before him the vision of that death of desolation which he should have to endure, forsaken by all, by men and by God, in the midst of a sea of sufferings and contempt. And this it was that caused him so heavy grief that he was obliged to pray for consolation to his eternal Father. O my Jesus! I compassionate Thee, I thank Thee, and I love Thee.

*And there appeared to Him an angel, . . . strengthening Him.*[1] Strength came, but, says the Venerable Bede, this rather increased than lightened his sufferings: "Strength did not diminish, but increased his sorrow." Yes, for the angel strengthened him, that he might suffer still more for the love of men and the glory of his Father.

Oh, what sufferings did not this first combat bring Thee, my beloved Lord! During the progress of Thy Passion, the scourges, the thorns, the nails, came one after the other to torment Thee. But in the garden all the sufferings of Thy whole Passion assaulted Thee all together and tormented Thee. And Thou didst accept all for my sake and my good. O my God! how much I regret not having loved Thee in times past, and having preferred my own accursed pleasures to Thy will! I detest them now above every evil, and repent of them with my whole heart. O my Jesus! forgive me.

III.

He, the Eternal Word, as much as he loved his Father, so much did he hate sin, of which he well knew the malice; wherefore, in order to deliver the world from sin, and that he might no longer behold his beloved Father offended, he had come upon earth, and had made himself Man, and had undertaken to suffer

---

[1] *Luke*, xxii. 43.

so painful a death and Passion. But when he saw that, notwithstanding all his sufferings, there would yet be so many sins committed in the world, his sorrow for this, says St. Thomas, exceeded the sorrow that any penitent has ever felt for his own sins.

We read in history that several penitents being enlightened by divine light to see the malice of their sins, have died of pure sorrow for them. Oh, what torment, then, must not the heart of Jesus endure at the sight of all the sins of the world, of all the blasphemies, sacrileges, acts of impurity, and all the other crimes which should be committed by men after his death, every one of which, like a wild beast, tore his heart separately by its own malice? Wherefore our afflicted Lord, during his agony in the garden, exclaimed, Is this, therefore, O men, the reward that you render me for my immeasurable love? Oh, if I could only see that, grateful for my affection, you gave up sin and began to love me, with what delight should I not hasten to die for you! But to behold, after all my sufferings, so many sins; after so much love, such ingratitude;—this is what afflicts me the most, makes me sorrowful even unto death, and makes me sweat pure blood: *And His sweat became as drops of blood trickling down upon the ground.*[1] So that, according to the Evangelist, this bloody sweat was so copious that it first bathed all the vestments of our Blessed Redeemer, and then came forth in quantity and bathed the ground.

---

[1] *Luke*, xxii. 44.

Ah, my loving Jesus, I do not behold in this garden either scourges or thorns or nails that pierce Thee; how, then, is it that I see Thee all bathed in blood from Thy head to Thy feet? Alas, my sins were the cruel press which, by dint of affliction and sorrow, drew so much blood from Thy heart. I was, then, one of Thy most cruel executioners, who contributed the most to crucify Thee with my sins. It is certain that, if I had sinned less, Thou, my Jesus, wouldst have suffered less. As much pleasure, therefore, as I have taken in offending Thee, so much the more did I increase the sorrow of Thy heart, already full of anguish. How, then, does not this thought make me die of grief, when I see that I have repaid the love Thou hast shown me in. Thy Passion by adding to Thy sorrow and suffering? I, then, have tormented this heart, so loving and so worthy of love, which has shown so much love to me. My Lord, since I have now no other means left of consoling Thee than to weep over my offences towards Thee, I will now, my Jesus, sorrow for them and lament over them with my whole heart. Oh, give me, I pray Thee, so great sorrow for them as may make me to my last breath weep over the displeasure I have caused Thee, my God, my Love my All.

IV.

*He fell upon His face.*[1] Jesus, beholding himself charged with the burden of satisfying for all the sins of the world, prostrated himself, with his face on the ground, to pray for men, as if he were ashamed to

[1] *Matt.* xxvi. 39.

raise his eyes towards heaven, loaded as he was with such iniquities.

O my Redeemer, I behold Thee pale and worn out with sorrow; Thou art in the agony of death, and Thou dost pray: *And being in an agony, He prayed the longer.*[1] Tell me, my Saviour, for whom dost Thou pray! Ah, Thou didst not pray so much for Thyself at that hour as for me! Thou didst offer to Thy Eternal Father Thy all-powerful prayers, united to Thy sufferings, to obtain for me, a wretched sinner, the pardon of my sins: *Who, in the days of His flesh, with a strong cry and tears, offering up prayers and supplications to Him that was able to save Him from death, was heard for His reverence.*[2] O my beloved Redeemer! how is it possible that Thou couldst love so much one who has so grievously offended Thee? How couldst Thou embrace such sufferings for me, foreseeing, as Thou didst, all the ingratitude of which I should be guilty towards Thee?

O my afflicted Lord! make me share in that sorrow which Thou didst then have for my sins. I abhor them at this present moment; and I unite this my hatred to the horror that Thou didst feel for them in the garden. O my Saviour, look not upon my sins, for hell itself would not be sufficient to expiate them, but look upon the sufferings that Thou hast endured for me! O my Lord, I love Thee with my whole soul, and will always love Thee. I beseech Thee, through the merits of that weariness and sadness which Thou

---

[1] *Luke*, xxii. 43.

[2] *Heb.* v. 7.

didst endure in the garden, give me fervor and courage in all works that may contribute to Thy glory. Through the merits of Thy agony, grant me Thy assistance to resist all the temptations of the flesh and of hell. My God, grant me the grace always to commend myself to Thee, and always to repeat to Thee, with Jesus Christ: *Not as I will, but as Thou willest.*[1] May Thy divine will, not mine, be ever done. Amen.

[1] *Mark*, xiv. 36.

# CHAPTER VII.

## THE LOVE OF JESUS IN SUFFERING SO MUCH CONTEMPT IN HIS PASSION.

### I.

Bellarmine says that to noble spirits affronts cause greater pain than sufferings of body: "Noble spirits think more of ignominy than of pains of body." Because, if the former afflict the flesh, the latter afflict the soul, which, in proportion as it is more noble than the body, so much the more does it feel pain.

And what kind of affronts did not the Redeemer suffer in his Passion? He saw himself affronted by his own disciples. One of them betrays him, and sells him for thirty pieces. Another denies him many times, protesting publicly that he knows him not; and thus attesting that he was ashamed to have known him in the past. The other disciples, then, at seeing him taken and bound, all fly and abandon him: *Then His disciples leaving Him, all fled away.*[1]

But, my God, to think that this dishonor did not end with Thy Passion! How many souls, after having devoted themselves to follow Thee, and after having been favored by Thee with many graces and special signs of love, being then driven by some passion of vile interest, or human respect, or sordid pleasure, have ungratefully forsaken Thee!

[1] *Mark*, xiv. 50.

Which of these ungrateful ones is found to turn and lament, saying, Ah, my dear Jesus, pardon me; for I will not leave Thee again. I will rather lose my life a thousand times than lose Thy grace, O my God, my love, my all.

II.

Behold how Judas, arriving in the garden together with the soldiers, advances, embraces his Master, and kisses him. Jesus suffers him to kiss him; but, knowing already his evil intent, could not refrain from complaining of this most unjust treachery, saying, *Judas, betrayest Thou the Son of man with a kiss?* [1] Then those insolent servants crowd around Jesus, lay hands upon him, and bind him as a villain.

Ah me! what do I see? A God bound! By whom? By men; by worms created by himself. Angels of paradise, what say ye to it? And Thou, my Jesus, why dost Thou allow Thyself to be bound? What, says St. Bernard, have the bonds of slaves and of the guilty to do with Thee, who art the Holy of Holies, the King of kings, and Lord of lords? "O King of kings and Lord of lords, what hast Thou to do with chains?"

But if men bind Thee, wherefore dost Thou not loosen and free Thyself from the torments and death which they are preparing for Thee? But I understand this. It is not, O my Lord, these ropes which bind Thee. It is only love which keeps Thee bound, and constrains Thee to suffer and die for us.

"O Charity," exclaims St. Laurence Justinian, "how strong is Thy chain, by which God was able to

---

[1] *John*, xviii. 12.

be bound!" O divine Love, thou only wast able to bind a God, and conduct him to death for the love of men.

III.

"Look, O man," says St. Bonaventure, "at these dogs dragging him along, and the Lamb, like a victim, meekly following without resistance." They carry our sweet Saviour, thus bound, first to the house of Annas, then to that of Caiphas; where Jesus, being asked by that wicked one about his disciples and his doctrine, replied that he had not spoken in private, but in public, and that they who were standing round about well knew what he had taught. *I spoke openly; lo, these know what I said.*[1] But at this answer one of those servants, treating him as if too bold, gave him a blow on the cheek: *One of the officers standing by gave Jesus a blow, saying, Answerest Thou the high-priest thus?*[2] Here exclaims St. Jerome: "Ye angels, how is it that ye are silent? How long can such patience withhold you in your astonishment?"

Ah, my Jesus, how could an answer so just and modest deserve such an affront in the presence of so many people? The worthless high-priest, instead of reproving the insolence of this audacious fellow, praises him, or at least by signs approves. And Thou, my Lord, sufferest all this to compensate for the affronts which I, a wretch, have offered to the divine

---

[1] *John*, xviii. 20.

[2] *Ibid.* 22.

Majesty by my sins. My Jesus, I thank Thee for it. Eternal Father, pardon me by the merits of Jesus.

IV.

Then the iniquitous high-priest asked him if he were verily the Son of God: *I adjure Thee by the living God, that Thou tell us if Thou be the Christ, the Son of God.*[1] Jesus, out of respect for the name of God, affirmed that he was so indeed; whereupon Caiphas rent his garments, saying that he had blasphemed; and all cried out that he deserved death: *But they answering said, He is guilty of death.*[2]

Yes, O my Jesus, with truth do they declare Thee guilty of death, since Thou hast willed to take upon Thee to make satisfaction for me, who deserved eternal death. But if by Thy death Thou hast acquired for me life, it is just that I should spend my life wholly, yea, and if need be lose it, for Thee. Yes, my Jesus, I will no longer live for myself; but only for Thee, and for Thy love. Succor me by Thy grace.

V.

*Then they spat in His face and buffeted Him.*[3] After having proclaimed him guilty of death, as a man already given over to punishment, and declared infamous, the rabble set themselves to ill-treat him all the night through with blows, and buffets, and kicks, with plucking out his beard, and even spitting in his face, by mocking him as a false prophet and saying,

---

[1] *Matt.* xxvi. 63

[2] *Ibid.* 66

[3] *Matt.* xxvi. 67.

*Prophesy to us, O Christ, who it is that struck Thee.*[1] All this our Redeemer foretold by Isaias: *I have given My body to the strikers, and my cheeks to them that plucked them: I have not turned away My face from them that rebuked Me and spit upon Me.*[2] The devout Thauler relates that it Is an opinion of St. Jerome that all the pains and infirmities which Jesus suffered on that night will be made known only on the day of the last judgment. St. Augustine, speaking of the ignominies suffered by Jesus Christ, says, "If this medicine cannot cure our pride, I know not what can." Ah, my Jesus, how is it that Thou art so humble and I so proud? O Lord, give me light, make me know who Thou art, and who I am.

Then they spat in His face. "Spat!" O God, what greater affront can there be than to be defiled by spitting? "To be spit upon is to suffer the extreme of insult," says Origen. Where are we wont to spit except in the most filthy place? And didst Thou, my Jesus, suffer Thyself to be spit upon in the face? Behold how these wretches outrage Thee; and dost Thou not threaten nor reprove them? *When He was reviled, He reviled not; when He suffered, He threatened not; but delivered Himself to him that judged Him unjustly.*[3] No, but like an innocent lamb, humble and meek, Thou didst suffer all without so much as complaining, offering all to the Father to obtain

---

1 *Ibid.* 68.

2 *Isa.* l. 6.

3 1 *Pet.* ii. 23.

the pardon of our sins: *Like a lamb before the shearer. He shall be dumb, and shall not open His mouth?* [1]

Ah, my reviled Lord, Thou art the King of heaven, the Son of the Most High; Thou surely deservest not to be ill-treated and despised, but to be adored and loved by all creatures. I adore Thee, I bless Thee, I thank Thee, I love Thee with all my heart. I repent of having offended Thee. Help me, have pity upon me.

VI.

When it was day, the Jews conduct Jesus to Pilate, to make him condemn him to death; but Pilate declares him to be innocent: *I find no cause in this Man.*[2] And to free himself from the importunities of the Jews pressed on him, seeking the death of the Saviour, he sends him to Herod. It greatly pleased Herod to see Jesus Christ brought before him, hoping that in his presence, in order to deliver himself from death, he would have worked one of those miracles of which he had heard tell; wherefore he asked him many questions. But Jesus, because he did not wish to be delivered from death, and because that wicked one was not worthy of his answers, was silent, and answered him not. Then the proud king, with his court, offered him many insults, and making them cover him with a white robe, as if declaring him to be an ignorant and stupid fellow, sent him back to Pilate: *But Herod with his soldiers despised Him, and mocked Him, putting on Him a white robe, and sent*

---

[1] *Isa.* liii. 7.

[2] *Luke*, xxiii. 4.

*Him back to Pilate.*[1] St. Bonaventure, in his Commentary, says, "He despised him as if impotent, because he worked no miracle; as if ignorant because he answered him not a word; as if idiotic, because he did not defend himself."

O Eternal Wisdom, O divine Word! This one other ignominy was wanting to Thee, that Thou shouldst be treated as a fool bereft of sense. So greatly does our salvation weigh on Thee, that through love of us Thou wiliest not only to be reviled, but to be satiated with revilings; as Jeremias had already prophesied of Thee: *He shall give His cheek to him that striketh Him; He shall be filled with reproaches.*[2] And how couldst Thou bear such love to men, from whom Thou hast received nothing but ingratitude and slights? Alas, that I should be one of these who have outraged Thee worse than Herod! Ah, my Jesus, chastise me not, like Herod, by depriving me of Thy voice. Herod did not recognize thee for what Thou art; I confess Thee to be my God. Herod loved Thee not; I love Thee more than myself. Deny me not I beseech Thee, deny me not the voice of Thy inspiration's I have deserved by the offences that I have committed against Thee. Tell me what Thou wilt have of me, for, by Thy grace, I am ready to do all that Thou wilt.

VII.

When Jesus had been led back to Pilate, the governor inquired of the people whom they wished to

---

[1] *Luke*, xxiii. 11.

[2] *Lam.* iii. 30

have released at that Passover, Jesus or Barabbas, a murderer. But the people cried out, *Not this Man, but Barabbas.*[1] Then said Pilate, *What then, shall I do with Jesus?*[2] They answered, *Let Him be crucified.*[3] But what evil hath this innocent one done? replied Pilate: *What evil hath he done?*[4] They repeated, *Let Him be crucified.*[5]

And even up to this time, O God, the greater part of mankind continue to say, *Not this Man, but Barabbas;*[6] preferring to Jesus Christ some pleasure of sense, some point of honor, some outbreak of wounded pride.

Ah, my Lord, well knowest Thou that at one time I did Thee the same injury when I preferred my accursed tastes to Thee. My Jesus, pardon me, for I repent of the past, and henceforth I prefer Thee before everything. I esteem Thee, I love Thee more than any good; and am willing a thousand times to die rather than forsake Thee. Give me holy perseverance; give me Thy love.

---

1 *John*, xviii. 40.
2 *Matt*, xxvii. 22.
3 *Ibid.*
4 *Ibid.* 23.
5 *Ibid.*
6 *John*, xviii. 40.

# CHAPTER VIII.

## THE SCOURGING OF JESUS CHRIST.

### I.

Let us enter into the prætorium of Pilate, one day made the horrible scene of the ignominies and pains of Jesus: let us see how unjust, how shameful, how cruel, was the punishment there inflicted on the Saviour of the world. Pilate, seeing that the Jews continued to make a tumult against Jesus, as a most unjust judge condemned him to be scourged: *Then Pilate took Jesus and scourged Him.*[1] The iniquitous judge thought by means of this barbarity to win for him the compassion of his enemies, and thus to deliver him from death: *I will chastise Him* (he said) *and let Him go.*[2] Scourging was the chastisement inflicted on slaves only. Therefore, says St. Bernard, our loving Redeemer willed to take the form, not only of a slave, in order to subject himself to the will of others, but even of a bad slave in order to be chastised with scourges, and so to pay the penalty due from man, who had made himself the slave of sin: "Taking not only the form of a slave, that he might submit, but even of a bad slave, that he might be beaten and suffer the punishment of the slave of sin."

---

[1] *John*, xix. 1.

[2] *Luke*, xxiii. 22.

A God scourged! It were a greater marvel that God should receive the lightest blow than that all men and all angels should be destroyed. Ah, my Jesus, pardon me the offences that I have committed against Thee, and then chastise me as shall please Thee. This alone is enough,—that I love Thee, and that Thou love me; and then I am content to suffer all the pains Thou wiliest.

II.

As soon as he had arrived at the prætorium (as was revealed to St. Bridget), our loving Saviour, at the command of the servants, stripped himself of his garments, embraced the column, and then laid on it his hands to have them bound. O angels of heaven, come and look on this sorrowful spectacle; and if it be not permitted you to deliver your king from this barbarous slaughter, at least come and weep for compassion.

And thou, my soul, imagine thyself to be present at this horrible tearing of the flesh of Thy beloved Redeemer. Look on him, how he stands,—thy afflicted Jesus,—with his head bowed, looking on the ground, blushing all over for shame, he awaits this great torture. Behold these barbarians, like so many ravening dogs, are already with the scourges attacking this innocent lamb. See how one beats him on the breast, another strikes his shoulders, another smites his loins and his legs; even his sacred head and his beautiful face cannot escape the blows.

Ah me! already flows that divine blood from every part; already with that blood are saturated the scourges, the hands of the executioners, the column, and the ground. "He is wounded," mourns St. Peter Damian, "over his whole body, torn with the scourges; now they twine round his shoulders, now round his legs—streaks upon streaks, wounds added to fresh wounds."

Ah, cruel men, with whom are you dealing thus? Stay—stay; know that you are mistaken. This man whom you are torturing is innocent and holy; it is myself who am the culprit; to me, to me, who have sinned, are these stripes and torments due. But you regard not what I say. And how canst Thou, O Eternal Father, bear with this great injustice? How canst Thou behold Thy beloved Son suffering thus, and not interfere in his behalf? What is the crime that he has ever committed, to deserve so shameful and so severe a punishment?

III.

*For the wickedness of My people have I struck Him.*[1] I well know, says the Eternal Father, that this my Son is innocent; but inasmuch as he has offered himself as a satisfaction to my justice for all the sins of mankind, it is fitting that I should so abandon him to the rage of his enemies.

Hast Thou, then, my adorable Saviour, in compensation for our sins, and especially for those of impurity,—that most prevalent vice of mankind,—been willing to have Thy most pure flesh torn in pieces? And who, then, will not exclaim, with St.

---

[1] *Isa.* liii. 8.

Bernard, "How unspeakable is the love of the Son of God towards sinners!"

Ah, my Lord, smitten with the scourge, I return Thee thanks for so great love, and I grieve that I am myself, by reason of my sins, one of those who scourge Thee. O my Jesus! I detest all those wicked pleasures which have cost Thee so much pain. Oh, how many years ought I not already to have been in the flames of hell! And why hast Thou so patiently awaited me until now? Thou hast borne with me, in order that at length, overcome by so many wiles of love, I might give myself up to love Thee, abandoning sin. O my beloved Redeemer! I will offer no further resistance to Thy loving affection; I desire to love Thee henceforth to the uttermost of my power. But Thou already knowest my weakness; Thou knowest how often I have betrayed Thee. Do Thou detach me from all earthly affections which hinder me from being all Thine own. Put me frequently in mind of the love which Thou hast borne me, and of the obligation which I am under of loving Thee. In Thee I place all my hopes, my God, my love, my all.

IV.

St. Bonaventure sorrowfully exclaims, "The royal blood is flowing; bruise is superadded to bruise, and gash to gash." That divine blood was already issuing from every pore; that sacred body was already become but one perfect wound; yet those infuriated brutes did not forbear to add blow to blow, as the Prophet had foretold: *And they have added to the grief of my wounds.*[1] So that the thongs not only made the whole body one wound, but even bore away pieces of it into the air, until at length the gashes in that sacred flesh were such that the bones might have been counted: *The flesh was so torn away, that the bones could be numbered.* Cornelius à Lapide says that in this torment Jesus Christ ought, naturally speaking, to have died; but he willed, by his divine power, to keep himself in life, in order to suffer yet greater pains for love of us; and St. Laurence Justinian had observed the same thing before: "He evidently ought to have died. Yet he reserved himself unto life, it being his will to endure heavier sufferings."

Ah, my most loving Lord, Thou hast suffered so much in order that I might love Thee. Oh, what place in hell should there not be set apart for me, if, after having known the love that Thou hast borne towards such a wretch, I should damn myself, despising a God who had suffered scorn, smitings, and scourgings for me; and who had, moreover, after my having so often offended him, so mercifully pardoned me! Ah, my Jesus, let it not, oh, let it not be thus! O my God! how would the love and the patience which Thou hast shown towards me be there for me in hell, another hell even yet more full of torments!

V.

Cruel in excess to our Redeemer was this torture of his scourging in the first place, because of the great number of those by whom it was inflicted; who, as

[1] *Ps.* lxviii. 27.

was revealed to St. Mary Magdalen of Pazzi, were not fewer than sixty. And these, at the instigation of the devils, and even more so of the priests, who were afraid lest Pilate should, after this punishment, be minded to release the Lord, as he had already protested to them, saying, *I will therefore scourge Him, and let Him go,*[1] aimed at taking away his life by means of this scourging. Again, all theologians agree with St. Bonaventure that, for this purpose, the sharpest implements were selected, so that, as St. Anselm declares, every stroke produced a wound; and that the number of the strokes amounted to several thousand, the flagellation being administered, as Father Crasset says, not after the manner of the Jews, for whom the Lord had forbidden that the number of strokes should ever exceed forty: *Yet so, that they exceed not the number of forty; lest thy brother depart shamefully torn,*[2] but after the manner of the Romans, with whom there was no measure.

And so it is related by Josephus, the Jew, who lived shortly after our Lord, that Jesus was torn in his scourging to such a degree that the bones of his ribs were laid bare; as it was also revealed by the most Holy Virgin to St. Bridget, in these words: "I, who was standing by, saw his body scourged to the very ribs, so that his ribs themselves might be seen. And what was even yet more bitter still, when the

---

[1] *Luke*, xxiii. 22.

[2] *Deut.* xxv. 3

scourges were drawn back, his flesh was furrowed by them."

Ah, my beloved and adored Jesus, how much hast Thou suffered for love of me! Oh, let not so many pangs, and so much blood, be lost for me!

VI.

But from the Scriptures alone it clearly appears how barbarous and inhuman was the scourging of Jesus Christ.

For why was it that Pilate should, after the scourging, ever have shown him to the people, saying, *Behold the Man!* [1] were it not that our Saviour was reduced to so pitiable a condition that Pilate believed the very sight of him would have moved his enemies themselves to compassion, and hindered them from any longer demanding his death?

Why was it that in the journey which Jesus, after this, made to Calvary, the Jews took the cross from off his shoulders, and gave it to the Cyrenian to carry? According to the most probable opinion, and as the words of St. Matthew clearly show, *they compelled him to bear His cross;* [2] or, as St. Luke says, *And on him they laid the cross, that he might carry it after Jesus.* [3] Was it, perhaps, that they felt pity for him and wished to lessen his pains? No, those guilty men hated him, and sought to afflict him to their uttermost. But, as the blessed Denis, the Carthusian, says, "they feared lest he should die upon the way,"

[1] *John*, xix. 5.
[2] *Matt.* xxvii. 32.
[3] *Luke*, xxiii. 26.

seeing that our Lord, after the scourging, was so drained of blood and so exhausted in strength as to be scarcely able any longer to stand, falling down as he did on his road under the cross, and faltering as he went, so to speak, at every step, as if at the point of death; therefore, in order to take him alive to Calvary and see him dead upon the cross, according to their desire, that his name might ever after be one of infamy: *Let us cut him off,* said they, as the Prophet had foretold, *from the land of the living, and let his name be remembered no more.*[1] This was the end for which they constrained the Cyrenian to bear the cross.

Ah, my Lord, great is my happiness in understanding how much Thou hast loved me, and that Thou dost even now preserve for me the same love that Thou didst bear me then, in the time of Thy Passion! By the merit of Thy scourging, O my Jesus, I ask Thy pardon, I repent, above every other evil, of having offended Thee; and I purpose rather to die than to offend Thee again. Pardon me all the wrongs that I have done Thee, and give me the grace ever to love Thee for the time to come.

VII.

Jesus one day manifested himself under his scourging to Sister Victoria Angelini; and showing her his body one mass of wounds, said to her, "These wounds, Victoria, every one of them, ask thee for love." "Let us love the Bridegroom," said the loving St. Augustine, "and the more he is presented to us

---

[1] *Jer.* xi. 19.

veiled under deformity, the more precious and sweet is he made to the bride."

Yes, my sweet Saviour, I see Thee all covered with wounds; I look into Thy beautiful face; but, O my God, it no longer wears its beautiful appearance, but disfigured and blackened with blood, and bruises, and shameful spittings: *There is no beauty in Him, nor comeliness: and we beheld Him, and esteemed Him not.*[1] But the more I see Thee so disfigured, O my Lord, the more beautiful and lovely dost Thou appear to me. And what are these disfigurements that I behold but signs of the tenderness of that love which Thou dost bear towards me? I love Thee, my Jesus, thus wounded and torn to pieces for me; would that I could see myself too torn to pieces for Thee, like so many martyrs whose portion this has been! But if I cannot offer Thee wounds and blood, I offer Thee at least all the pains which it will be my lot to suffer. I offer Thee my heart; with this I desire to love Thee more tenderly even than I am able. I love Thee, O my love, my all! I love Thee, and I would never cease to say, both in this life and in the other, I love Thee, I love Thee, I love Thee. Amen.

---

[1] *Isa.* liii. 2.

# CHAPTER IX.

## THE CROWNING WITH THORNS.

### I.

As the soldiers, however, perseveringly continued their cruel scourging of the innocent Lamb, it is related that one of those who were standing by came forward, and, taking courage, said to them, You have no orders to kill this man, as you are trying to do. And, saying this, he cut the cords wherewith the Lord was standing bound. This was revealed to St. Bridget: "Then a certain man, his spirit being moved within him, demanded, Are you going to kill him in this manner, uncondemned? and forthwith he cut his bonds."

But hardly was the scourging ended, when those barbarous men, urged on and bribed by the Jews with money, as St. John Chrysostom avers, inflict upon the Redeemer a fresh kind of torture: *Then the soldiers of the governor taking Jesus into the prætorium, gathered together the whole band, and stripped Him, clothed Him in a purple robe, and platting a crown of thorns, they put it upon His head, and a reed in His right hand.*[1] Behold how the soldiers strip him again; and, treating him as a mock king, place upon him a purple garment, which was nothing else but a ragged cloak, one of those that were worn by the

[1] *Matt.* xxvii. 27-30.

Roman soldiers, and called a chlamys; in his hand they place a reed to represent a sceptre, and upon his head a bundle of thorns to represent a crown.

Ah, my Jesus, and art not Thou, then, true king of the universe? And how is it that Thou art now become king of sorrow and reproach? See whither love has brought Thee! O Lord, as long as I live in this world, I always stand in danger of turning my back upon Thee, and of refusing to Thee my love, as I have unhappily done in time past. O my Jesus, if Thou foreseest that by continuing in life I should have to suffer this greatest of all misfortunes, let me die at this moment, while I hope that I am in Thy grace! I pray Thee, by Thy Passion, not to abandon me to so great an evil. I should indeed deserve it for my sins; but Thou dost deserve it not. Choose out any punishment for me rather than this. No, my Jesus, my Jesus, I would not see myself ever again separated from Thee.

II.

*And platting a crown of thorns, they put it upon His head.*[1] It was a good reflection of the devout Lanspergius, that this torture of the crown of thorns was one most full of pain; inasmuch as they everywhere pierced into the sacred head of the Lord, the most sensitive part, it being from the head that all the nerves and sensations of the body diverge; while it was also that torture of his Passion which lasted the longest, as Jesus suffered from the thorns up to his death, remaining, as they did, fixed in his head.

[1] *Matt.* xxvii. 29.

Every time that the thorns on his head were touched, the anguish was renewed afresh. And the common opinion of authors agrees with that of St. Vincent Ferrer, that the crown was intertwined with several branches of thorns, and fashioned like a helmet or hat, so that it fitted upon the whole of the head, down to the middle of the forehead; according to the revelation made to St. Bridget: "The crown of thorns embraced his head most tightly, and came down as low as the middle of the forehead."

While the gentle Lamb let himself be tormented according to their will, without speaking a word, without crying out, but compressing his eyes together through the anguish, he frequently breathed forth, at that time, bitter sighs, as is the wont of one undergoing a torture which has brought him to the point of death, according as was revealed to the Blessed Agatha of the Cross: "He very often closed his eyes, and uttered piercing sighs, like those of one about to die." So great was the quantity of the blood which flowed from the wounds upon his sacred head, that upon his face there was no appearance of any other color save that of blood, according to the revelation of St. Bridget: "So many streams of blood rushing down over his face, and filling his hair, and eyes, and beard, he seemed to be nothing but one mass of blood." And St. Bonaventure adds, that the beautiful face of the Lord was no longer seen, but it appeared rather the face of a man who had been scarified: "Then might be seen no longer the face of the Lord Jesus, but that of a man who had undergone excoriation."

"O love!" exclaims Salvian, "what to call Thee I know not, sweet or cruel. Thou seemest to be both." Ah, my Jesus, true, indeed, it is that love makes Thee sweet, as regards us, showing Thee forth to us as so passionate a lover of our souls; but it makes Thee pitiless towards Thyself, causing Thee to suffer such bitter torments. Thou wast willing to be crowned with thorns to obtain for us a crown of glory in heaven. O my sweetest Saviour, I hope to be Thy crown in paradise, obtaining my salvation through the merits of Thy sufferings; there will I forever praise Thy love and Thy mercies: *The mercies of the Lord will I forever sing; yea, I will sing them forever.*[1]

III.

Ah, cruel thorns, ungrateful creatures, wherefore do ye torment your Creator thus? But to what purpose, asks St. Augustine, dost thou find fault with the thorns? They were but innocent instruments—our sins, our evil thoughts, were the wicked thorns which afflicted the head of Jesus Christ: "What are the thorns but sinners?" Jesus having one day appeared to St. Teresa crowned with thorns, the saint began to compassionate him; but the Lord made answer to her: "Teresa, compassionate me not on account of the wounds which the thorns of the Jews produced; but commiserate me on account of the wounds which the sins of Christians occasion me." Thou, too, therefore, O my soul, didst then indict torture upon the venerable head of thy Redeemer by thy many consentings to evil: *Know thou and behold how*

---

[1] *Ps.* lxxxviii. 2.

*grievous and bitter it is for thee to have left the Lord thy God.*[1] Open now thine eyes, and see, and bitterly bewail all thy life long the evil that thou hast done in so ungratefully turning thy back upon thy Lord and God.

Ah, my Jesus! no, Thou hast not deserved that I should have treated Thee as I have done. I have done evil; I have been in the wrong; I am sorry for it with all my heart. Oh, pardon me, and give me a sorrow which may make me bewail all my life long the wrongs that I have done Thee. My Jesus, my Jesus, pardon me, wishing, as I do, to love Thee forever.

IV.

*And bowing the knee before Him, they derided Him, saying, Hail, King of the Jews: and spitting upon Him, they took a reed, and smote Him upon the head.*[2] St. John adds, *And they gave Him blows.*[3] When those barbarians had placed upon the head of Jesus that crown of torture, it was not enough for them to press it down as forcibly as they could with their hands, but they took a reed to answer the purpose of a hammer, that so they might make the thorns penetrate the more deeply. Ah, my Jesus, to what art Thou reduced!

Had any one happened by chance to pass that place and seen Jesus Christ so drained of blood, clad in that ragged purple garment, with that sceptre in his hand, with that crown upon his head, and so

---

[1] *Jer.* ii. 19.

[2] *Matt.* xxvii. 29.

[3] *John*, xix. 3.

derided and ill-treated by that low rabble, what would he ever have taken him to be but the vilest and most wicked man in the world! Behold the Son of God become at that time the disgrace of Jerusalem!

Ah, my dear Redeemer, take back a rebellious servant who has run away from Thee, but who now returns to Thee in penitence. While I was fleeing from Thee and despising Thy love, Thou didst not cease from following after me to draw me back to Thyself; and therefore I cannot fear that Thou wilt drive me away now that I seek Thee, value Thee, and love Thee above everything. Make known to me what I have to do to please Thee. O my most lovely God, I wish to love Thee in earnest; and I desire to give Thee no displeasure more. Aid me with Thy grace. Let me not leave Thee more. Mary, my hope, pray to Jesus for me. Amen.

# CHAPTER X.

## "ECCE HOMO"— "BEHOLD THE MAN."

### I.

Pilate, seeing the Redeemer reduced to that condition, so moving, as it was, to compassion, thought that the mere sight of him would have softened the Jews. He therefore led him forth into the balcony; he raised up the purple garment, and, exhibiting to the people the body of Jesus all covered with wounds and gashes, he said to them, Behold the man: *Pilate went forth again to them, and saith to them: Behold, I am bringing Him out to you, that you may know that I find no fault in Him. Jesus, therefore, went forth, wearing the crown of thorns and the purple garment; and he saith unto them, Behold the Man.*[1] *Behold the Man!* as though he would have said, I, to please you, have sentenced him, innocent although he be, to be scourged: "Behold the Man, not honored as a king, but covered with disgrace." Behold him now, reduced to such a state that he wears the appearance of a man that has been flayed alive; and he can have but little life left in him. If, with all this, you want me to condemn him to death, I tell you that I cannot do so, as I find not any reason for condemning him. But the Jews on beholding Jesus thus ill-treated, waxed more fierce: *When, therefore, the chief priests and the*

[1] *John*, xix. 4,5.

*officers saw Him, they cried out, saying, Crucify Him! crucify Him!* [1] Pilate, seeing that they could not be pacified, washed his hands in the presence of the people, saying, *I am innocent of the blood of this just Man; look you to it.*[2] And they made answer, *His blood be upon us, and upon our children.*[3]

O my beloved Saviour! Thou art the greatest of all kings; yet now I behold Thee the most reviled of all mankind. If this ungrateful people knows Thee not, I know Thee; and I adore Thee as my true King and Lord. I thank Thee, O my Redeemer, I blush at having in time past loved honors and pleasures so much, that for their sake I have often gone so far as to renounce Thy grace and Thy love. I repent of this above every other evil. I embrace, O Lord, all the pains and ignominies that will come to me from Thy hands. Do Thou bestow upon me that resignation which I need. I love Thee, my Jesus, my love, my all.

II.

But while Pilate from the balcony was exhibiting Jesus to that populace, at the self-same time the Eternal Father from heaven was presenting to us his beloved Son, saying, in like manner, *Behold the Man.* Behold this Man, who is my only-begotten Son, whom I love with the same love wherewith I love myself: *This is My beloved Son, in whom I am well pleased.*[4] Behold the Man, your Saviour, him whom

---

[1] *John*, xix. 6.
[2] *Matt.* xxvii. 24.
[3] *Ibid.* 25.
[4] *Matt.* iii. 17.

I promised, and for whom you were anxiously waiting. Behold the Man, who is nobler than all other men, become the man of sorrows. Behold him, and see to what a pitiable condition he has reduced himself through the love which he has borne towards you, and in order to be, at least out of compassion, beloved by you again. Oh, look at him, and love him; and if his great worth move you not, at least let these sorrows and ignominies which he suffers for you move you to love him.

Ah, my God and Father of my Redeemer! I love Thy Son, who suffers for love of me; and I love Thee, who with so much love hast abandoned him to so many pains for me. Oh, look not on my sins by which I have so often offended Thee and Thy Son: *Look upon the face of Thy Christ.*[1] Behold Thine only-begotten, all covered with wounds and shame in satisfaction for my faults; and for his merits pardon me, and never let me again offend Thee. *His blood be upon us.* The blood of this man, so dear unto Thee, who prays to Thee for us, and impetrates Thy mercy, let this descend upon our souls, and obtain for us Thy grace. O my Lord! I hate and abhor all that I have done that displeases Thee; and I love Thee, O infinite goodness, more than I love myself. For love of this Thy Son give me Thy love, to enable me to conquer every passion, and to undergo every suffering in order to please Thee.

[1] *Ps.* lxxxiii, 10.

III.

*Go forth, ye daughters of Sion, and behold King Solomon in his crown, wherewith his mother crowned him on the day of his espousals, and on the day of the joy of his heart.*[1] Go forth, ye souls redeemed, ye daughters of grace, go forth to see your gentle king, on the day of his death, the day of his joy, for thereon he made you his spouses, giving up his life upon the cross, crowned by the ungrateful synagogue, his mother, with a crown; not indeed one of honor, but one of suffering and shame: "Go forth," says St. Bernard, "and behold your king in a crown of poverty and misery."

O most beautiful of all mankind! O greatest of all monarchs! O most lovely of all spouses! to what a state do I see Thee reduced, covered with wounds and contempt! Thou art a spouse, but a spouse of blood: *To me Thou art a spouse of blood;*[2] it being by means of Thy blood that Thou hast willed to espouse Thyself to our souls. Thou art a king, but a king of suffering and a king of love; it being by sufferings that Thou hast willed to gain our affections.

O most beloved spouse of my soul! would that I were continually recalling to my mind how much Thou hast suffered for me, that so I might never cease to love and please Thee! O my beloved Jesus! give me more love, if Thou wouldst that I should love Thee more. I desire to have a very great love for Thee.

---

[1] *Cant.* iii. 11.

[2] *Exod.* iv. 25.

So wretched a sinner as I am ought to have been burning in hell ever since the moment in which I first gravely offended Thee; but Thou hast borne with me even until this hour, because Thou dost not wish me to burn with that miserable fire, but with the blessed fire of Thy love. This thought, O God of my soul, sets me all in flame with the desire of doing all that I can to please Thee. Help me, O my Jesus; and since Thou hast done so much, complete the work, and make me wholly Thine.

IV.

But the Jews going on to insult the governor, crying out, *Away with Him! away with Him! crucify Him!* [1] Pilate said to them, *Shall I crucify your King?* and they made answer, *We have no king but Cæsar.*[2] The worldly-minded, who love the riches, the honors, and the pleasures of earth, refuse to have Jesus Christ for their king; because, as far as this earth is concerned, Jesus was but a king of poverty, shame, and sufferings.

But if such as these refuse Thee, O my Jesus, we choose Thee for our only king, and we make our protestation that "we have no king but Jesus." Yes, most lovely Saviour, *Thou art my king;*[3] Thou art and hast forever to be my only Lord. True king, indeed, art Thou of our souls; for Thou hast created them, and redeemed them from the slavery of Satan: *Thy kingdom come.* Exercise, then, Thy dominion, and reign

---

[1] *John*, xix. 15.

[2] *Ibid.*

[3] *Ps.* xliii. 5.

forever in our poor hearts; may they ever serve and obey Thee! Be it for others to serve the monarchs of earth, in hope of the good things of this world. Our desire it is to serve only Thee, our afflicted and despised king, in hope only of pleasing Thee, without any earthly consolations. Dear to us, from this day forth, shall shame and sufferings be, since Thou hast been willing to endure so much of them for love of us. Oh, grant us the grace to be faithful unto Thee; and to this end bestow upon us the great gift of Thy love. If we love Thee, we shall also love the contempt and the sufferings which were so much beloved by Thee; and we shall ask Thee for nothing but that which Thy faithful and loving servant St. John of the Cross asked of Thee: "Lord, to suffer and be despised for Thee; Lord, to suffer and be despised for Thee!" O Mary, my Mother, intercede for me. Amen.

# CHAPTER XI.

## THE CONDEMNATION OF JESUS CHRIST, AND HIS JOURNEY TO CALVARY.

### I.

Pilate was going on making excuses to the Jews, to the effect that he could not condemn that innocent One to death, when they worked upon his fears by telling him: *If thou lettest this Man go, thou art no friend of Caesar's.*[1] And hence the miserable judge, blinded by the fear of losing Caesar's favor, after having so often recognized and declared the innocence of Jesus Christ, at last condemned him to die by crucifixion: *Then he delivered Him up to them, that He might be crucified.*[2]

O my beloved Redeemer (St. Bernard hereupon bewails), what crime hast Thou committed that Thou shouldst have to be condemned to death, and that death the death of the cross? Ah, I well understand, replies the saint, the reason for Thy death; I understand what has been Thy crime: "Thy crime is Thy love." Thy crime is the too great love which Thou hast borne to men; it is this, not Pilate, that condemns Thee to die. No, adds St. Bonaventure, I see no just reason for Thy death, O my Jesus, save the excess of the affection which Thou bearest to us: "I see no cause for death but the superabundance of love." Ah,

[1] *John*, xix. 12.
[2] *Ibid.* 16.

so great an excess of love, goes on St. Bernard, how strongly does it constrain us, O loving Saviour, to consecrate all the affections of our hearts unto Thee! "Such love wholly claims for itself our love."

O my dear Saviour, the mere knowledge that Thou dost love me should be sufficient to make me live detached from everything, in order to study only how to love Thee and please Thee in all things: *Love is strong as death.*[1] If love is as strong as death, oh, by Thy merits, my Saviour, grant me such a love for Thee as shall make me hold all earthly affections in abhorrence. Give me thoroughly to understand that all my good consists in pleasing Thee, O God, all goodness and all love! I curse that time in which I loved Thee not. I thank Thee for that Thou dost give me time in which to love. With my whole self do I love Thee, and I assure Thee that I would wish to die a thousand deaths rather than ever again cease from loving Thee.

II.

The unjust sentence of death is read over to Jesus, who stands condemned; he listens to it, and humbly accepts it. No complaint does he make of the injustice of the judge; no appeal does he make to Cæsar, as did St. Paul, but, all gentle and resigned, he submits himself to the decree of the Eternal Father, who condemns him to the cross for our sins: *He humbled Himself, being made obedient even unto death, and that the death of the cross.*[2] And, for the love which

---

[1] *Cant.* viii. 6.

[2] *Phil.* ii. 8.

he bears to man, he is content to die for us: *He loved us, and gave Himself up for us.*[1]

O my merciful Saviour, how much do I thank Thee! How deeply am I obliged to Thee! I desire, O my Jesus, to die for Thee, since Thou hast so lovingly accepted of death for me. But if it is not granted me to give Thee my blood and life at the hands of the executioner, as the Martyrs have done, I, at least, accept with resignation the death which awaits me; and I accept of it in the manner, and at the time, which shall please Thee. Henceforth do I offer it up to Thee in honor of Thy Majesty, and in satisfaction for my sins. I pray Thee, by the merits of Thy death, to grant me the happiness to die in Thy grace and love.

III.

Pilate delivers over the innocent Lamb into the hands of those wolves, to do with him what they will: *But he delivered Jesus up to their will.*[2] These ministers of Satan seize hold of him fiercely; they strip him of the purple garment, as is suggested to them by the Jews, and put his own raiment again upon him: *They stripped Him of the purple garment, and clothed Him in His own raiment, and led Him away to crucify Him.*[3] And this they did, says St. Ambrose, in order that Jesus might be recognized, at least, by his apparel; his beautiful face being so much disfigured with blood and wounds, that in other apparel it

[1] *Eph.* v. 2.
[2] *Luke*, xxii. 25.
[3] *Matt.* xxvii. 31.

would have been difficult for him to have been recognized as the person he was: "They put on him his own raiment, that he might the better be recognized by all; since, as his face was all bloody and disfigured, it would not have been an easy matter for all to have recognized him." They then take two rough beams, and of them they quickly construct the cross, the length of which was fifteen feet, as St. Bonaventure says, with St. Anselm, and they lay it upon the shoulders of the Redeemer.

But Jesus did not wait, says St. Thomas of Villanova, for the executioner to lay the cross upon him; of his own accord he stretched forth his hands, and eagerly laid hold of it, and placed it upon his own wounded shoulders: "He waited not till the soldier should lay it upon him, but he grasped hold of it joyfully." Come, he then said, come, my beloved cross; it is now three-and-thirty years that I am sighing and searching for thee. I embrace thee, I clasp thee to my heart, for thou art the altar upon which it is my will to sacrifice my life out of love for my flock.

Ah, my Lord, how couldst Thou do so much good to one who has done Thee so much evil? O God, when I think of Thy having gone so far as to die under torments to obtain for me the divine friendship, and that I have so often voluntarily lost it afterwards through my own fault, I would that I could die of grief! How often hast Thou forgiven me, and I have gone back and offended Thee again! How could I ever have hoped for pardon, were it not that I knew that Thou hast died in order to pardon me? By this Thy death, then, I hope for pardon, and for perseverance in loving Thee. I repent, O my Redeemer, of having offended Thee. By Thy merits, pardon me, who promise never to displease Thee more. I prize and love Thy friendship more than all the good things of this world. Oh, let it not be my lot to go back and lose it! Inflict me, O Lord, with any punishment rather than with this. O my Jesus, I am not willing to lose Thee any more; no, I would sooner be willing to lose my life: I wish to love Thee always.

IV.

The officers of justice come forth with the criminals condemned; and in the midst of these also moves forward unto death the King of heaven, the only-begotten Son of God, laden with his cross: *And bearing His own cross, He went forth to that place which is called Calvary.*[1] Do ye too, O blessed Seraphim, sally forth from heaven, and come and accompany your Lord, who is going to Calvary, there to be executed, together with the malefactors, upon a gibbet of infamy.

O horrifying sight! A God executed! Behold that Messias who but a few days before had been proclaimed the Saviour of the world, and received with acclamations and benedictions by the people, who cried out, *Hosanna to the Son of David; blessed be He that cometh in the name of the Lord;*[2] and, after all, to see him as, bound, ridiculed, and execrated by all, he moves along, laden with a cross, to die the death

---

[1] *John*, xix. 17.

[2] *Matt.* xxi. 9.

of a villain! A God executed for men! And shall we find any man who loves not this God?

O my Eternal Lover, late is it that I begin to love Thee: grant that during the remainder of my life, I may make amends for the time that I have lost. I know, indeed, that all that I can do is but little in comparison with the love which Thou hast borne me; but it is at least my wish to love Thee with my whole heart. Too great a wrong should I be doing Thee if, after so many kindnesses, I were to divide my heart in twain, and give a part of it to some object other than Thyself. From this day forth I consecrate unto Thee all my life, my will, my liberty: dispose of me as Thou pleasest. I beg paradise of Thee, that there I may love Thee with all my strength. I wish to love Thee exceedingly in this life, that I may love Thee exceedingly for all eternity Aid me by Thy grace: this I beg of Thee, and hope for, through Thy merits.

V.

Imagine to thyself, O my soul, that thou meetest Jesus as he passes along in this sorrowful journey. As a lamb borne along to the slaughter-house, so is the loving Redeemer conducted unto death: *As a lamb He is led to the slaughter.*[1] So drained of blood is he and wearied out with his torments, that for very weakness he can scarcely stand. Behold him, all torn with wounds, with that bundle of thorns upon his head, with that heavy cross upon his shoulders, and with one of those soldiers dragging him along by a rope. Look at him as he goes along, with body bent

---

[1] *Isa.* liii. 7.

double, with knees all of a tremble, dripping with blood; and so painful is it to him to walk, that at every step he seems ready to die.

Put the question to him: O divine lamb, hast Thou not yet had Thy fill of sufferings? If it is by them that Thou dost aim at gaining my love, oh, let Thy sufferings end here, for I wish to love Thee as Thou dost desire. No, he replies, I am not yet content: then shall I be content when I see myself die for love of you. And whither, O my Jesus, art Thou going now? I am going, he answers, to die for you. Hinder me not: this only do I ask of, and recommend to, you, that, when you shall see me actually dead upon the cross for you, you will keep in mind the love which I have borne you; bear it in mind, and love me.

O my afflicted Lord, how dear did it cost Thee to make me comprehend the love which Thou hast had for me! But what benefit could ever have resulted to Thee from my love, that Thou hast been willing to expend Thy blood and Thy life to gain it? And how could I, after having been bound by so great love, have been able so long to live without loving Thee, and unmindful of Thy affection? I thank Thee, for that now Thou dost give me light to make me know how much Thou hast loved me. O infinite goodness I love Thee above every good. Bestow upon me that sacred fire which Thou didst come to enkindle upon earth by dying for us. Be ever reminding me of Thy death, that I may never forget to love Thee.

VI.

*His government was upon His shoulder.*[1] The cross, says Tertullian, was precisely the noble instrument whereby Jesus Christ made acquisition of so many souls; since, by dying thereon, he paid the penalty due to our sins, and thus rescued us from hell, and made us his own. *Who His own Self bore our sins in His body upon the tree.*[2]

If God, then, O my Jesus, burdened Thee with all the sins of men—*The Lord laid upon Him the iniquities of us all,*[3]—I, with my own sins, added to the weight of the cross that Thou didst bear to Calvary. Ah, my sweetest Saviour, Thou didst even then foresee all the wrongs that I should do Thee; yet, notwithstanding, Thou didst not cease to love me, or to prepare for me all the mercies that Thou hast since employed towards me. If, then, to Thee I have been dear, most vile and ungrateful sinner as I am, who have so much offended Thee, good reason is there why Thou shouldst be dear to me,—Thou, my God, infinite in beauty and goodness, who hast loved me so much. Ah, would that I had never displeased Thee! Now, my Jesus, do I know the wrong that I have done Thee. O ye accursed sins of mine, what have you done? You have caused me to sadden the loving heart of my Redeemer, that heart which has loved me so much. O my Jesus, forgive me, repenting,

[1] *Isa.* ix. 6.
[2] 1 *Pet.* ii. 24.
[3] *Isa.* liii. 6.

as I do, of having done despite unto Thee. Henceforth it is Thou who art to be the only object of my love. I love Thee, O infinite loveliness, with all my heart; and I resolve to love none else but Thee. Pardon me, O Lord, and give me Thy love; I ask Thee for nothing more: "Give me Thy love only together with Thy grace" (I say unto Thee with St. Ignatius), "and I am rich enough."

VII.

*If any man will come after Me, let him deny himself and follow Me.*[1] Since, then, O my Redeemer, Thou dost go before me with Thy cross, innocent as Thou art, and dost invite me to follow Thee with mine, go forward, for I will not abandon Thee. If, in time past, I have abandoned Thee, I confess that I have done wrong. Give me now what Thou wilt, embracing it, as I do, whatsoever it be, and willing, as I am, to accompany Thee with it even unto death: *Let us go forth from the camp, bearing His reproach.*[2] But since Thou dost invite us to follow Thee, yea, it is our wish to follow Thee and to die with Thee: give us only the strength to carry it out. This strength we ask of Thee, and hope for by Thy merits. I love Thee, O my most lovely Jesus, I love Thee with all my soul, and I will never abandon Thee more; enough for me has been the time that I have gone astray from Thee. Bind me now to Thy cross. If I have despised Thy love, I repent of it with all my heart; and I now prize it above every good.

---

[1] *Matt.* xvi. 24.

[2] *Heb.* xiii. 13.

Ah, my Jesus, and who am I that thou wishest to have me for a follower of Thine, and commandest me to love Thee, and if I will not love Thee, threatenest me with hell? And why, I will say to Thee, with St. Augustine, shouldst Thou hold out to me the threat of eternal miseries? For what greater misery could befall me than that of not loving Thee, O most lovely God, my Creator, my Redeemer, my paradise, my all? I see that, as a just chastisement of my offences against Thee, I should have deserved to be condemned to the inability of ever loving Thee more; but because Thou dost still love me, Thou dost continue to command me to love Thee, evermore repeating to my heart, *Thou shalt love the Lord Thy God with all thy heart, with all thy soul, and with all thy mind.*[1] I thank Thee, O my love, for this sweet precept; and in order to obey Thee, I do love Thee with all my heart, with all my soul, and with all my mind. I repent of not having loved Thee in time past. At this moment I would rather choose to undergo every suffering than live without loving Thee, and I purpose evermore to seek Thy love. Help me, O my Jesus, to be ever making acts of love towards Thee, and to depart out of this life while making an act of love, that so I may come to love Thee, face to face, in Paradise, where I shall ever after love Thee without imperfection and without interruption, with all my powers, for all eternity. O Mother of God, pray for me. Amen.

[1] *Matt.* xxii. 37.

## CHAPTER XII.

### THE CRUCIFIXION OF JESUS.

I.

Behold, here we are at the Crucifixion, at that last torture, which brought death to Jesus Christ; here we are at Calvary, converted into a theatre for the display of divine love, where a God departs this life in an ocean of sufferings: *And when they had come to the place which is called Calvary, they crucified Him there.*[1] The Lord having, with great difficulty, at length reached the top of the Mount alive, they violently, for the third time, tear his clothes from off him, sticking, as they did, to the sores upon his wounded flesh, and they throw him down upon the cross. The divine lamb stretches himself out upon that bed of torment; he reaches forth to the executioners his hands and his feet to be nailed; and raising his eyes to heaven, he offers up to his Eternal Father the great sacrifice of his life for the salvation of men. After the nailing of one of his hands, the nerves shrink, so that they had need of force and ropes, as was revealed by St. Bridget, to draw the other hand and the feet up to the places where they were to be nailed; and this occasioned so great a tension of the nerves and veins, that they broke asunder with a violent convulsion: "They drew my hands and

[1] *Luke*, xxiii. 33.

my feet with a rope to the places of the nails, so that the nerves and veins were stretched out to the full and broke asunder;" inasmuch that all his bones might have been numbered, as David had already predicted: *They pierced My hands and My feet, they numbered all My bones.*[1]

Ah, my Jesus, by what power was it that Thy hands and Thy feet were nailed to this wood, but by the love Thou didst bear to men? Thou, by the pain of Thy pierced hands, wert willing to pay the penalty due to all the sins of touch that men have committed; and, by the pain of Thy feet, Thou wert willing to pay for all the steps by which we have gone our way to offend Thee. O my crucified love, with these pierced hands give me Thy benediction! Oh, nail this ungrateful heart of mine to Thy feet, that so I may no more depart from Thee, and that this will of mine, which has so often rebelled against Thee, may remain ever steadily fixed in Thy love. Grant that nothing else but Thy love, and the desire of pleasing Thee may move me. Although I behold Thee suspended upon this gibbet, I believe Thee to be the Lord of the world, the true Son of God, and the Saviour of mankind. For pity's sake, O my Jesus, never abandon me again at any period of my life; and more especially at the hour of my death, in those last agonies and struggles with hell, do Thou assist me, and strengthen me to die in Thy love. I love Thee, my crucified love, I love Thee with all my heart.

---

[1] *Ps.* xxi. 17.

II.

St Augustine says, there is no death more bitter than that of the cross: "Among all the different kinds of death, there was none worse." Because, as St. Thomas observes, those who are crucified have their hands and their feet pierced through, parts which, being entirely composed of nerves, muscles, and veins, are the most sensitive to pain; and the very weight of the body itself, which is suspended from them, causes the pain to be continuous and ever increasing in its intensity up to the moment of death.

But the pains of Jesus were far beyond all other pains; for, as the Angelic Doctor says, the body of Jesus Christ, being perfectly constituted, was more quick and sensitive to pain—that body which was fashioned for him by the Holy Spirit, expressly with a view to his suffering, as he had foretold; as the Apostle testifies, *A body thou hast fitted to Me.*[1] Moreover, St. Thomas says that Jesus Christ took upon himself an amount of suffering so great as to be sufficient to satisfy for the temporal punishment merited by the sins of all mankind. Tiepoli tells us that, in the crucifixion, there were dealt twenty-eight strokes of the hammer upon his hands, and thirty-six upon his feet.

O my soul, behold thy Lord, behold thy life, hanging upon that tree: *And thy life shall be, as it were, hanging before thee.*[2] Behold how, on that gibbet of

[1] *Heb*. x. 5.

[2] *Deut*. xxviii. 66.

pain, fastened by those cruel nails, he finds no place of rest. Now he leans his weight upon his hands, now upon his feet; but on what part soever he leans, the anguish increases. He turns his afflicted head, now on one side, now on the other: if he lets it fall towards his breast, the hands, by the additional weight, are rent the more; if he lowers it towards his shoulders, the shoulders are pierced with the thorns; if he leans it back upon the cross, the thorns enter the more deeply into the head.

Ah, my Jesus, what a death of bitterness is this that Thou art enduring! O my crucified Redeemer, I adore Thee on this throne of ignominy and pain. Upon this cross I read it written that Thou art a king: *Jesus of Nazareth, King of the Jews.*[1] But apart from this title of scorn, what is the evidence that Thou dost give of being a king? Ah, these hands transfixed with nails, this head pierced with thorns, this throne of sorrow, this lacerated flesh, make me well know that Thou art king, but king of love! With humility, then, and tenderness do I draw near to kiss Thy sacred feet, transfixed for love of me; I clasp in my arms this cross, on which Thou, being made a victim of love, wast willing to offer Thyself in sacrifice for me to the divine justice: *being made obedient unto death, the death of the cross.*[2] O blessed obedience which obtained for us the pardon of our sins! And what would have become of me, O my Saviour, hadst Thou not paid the penalty for me! I thank Thee O my love, and

---

[1] *John*, xix. 19.
[2] *Phil.* ii. 8.

by the merits of this sublime obedience do I pray Thee to grant me the grace of obedience in everything to the divine will. All that I desire paradise for is, that I may love Thee forever, and with all my strength.

III.

Behold the King of heaven, who, hanging on that gibbet, is now on the point of giving up the ghost. Let us, too, ask of him, with the prophet: *What are those wounds in the middle of Thy hands?* [1] Tell me, O my Jesus, what are these wounds in the middle of Thy hands? The Abbot Rupert makes answer for Jesus: "They are the memorials of charity, the price of redemption." They are tokens, says the Redeemer, of the great love which I bear towards you; they are the payment by which I set you free from the hands of your enemies, and from eternal death.

Do thou, then, O faithful soul, love thy God, who hath had such love for thee; and if thou dost at any time feel doubtful of his love, turn thine eyes (says St. Thomas of Villanova)—turn thine eyes to behold that cross, those pains, and that bitter death which he has suffered for thee; for such proofs will assuredly make thee know how much thy Redeemer loves thee: "The cross testifies, the pains testify, the bitter death which he had endured for thee testifies this." And St. Bernard adds that the cross cries out, every wound of Jesus cries out, that he loves us with a true love: "The cross proclaims, the wounds proclaim, that he truly loves."

---

[1] *Zach.* xiii. 6.

O my Jesus! how do I behold Thee weighed down with sorrow and sadness! Ah, too much reason hast Thou to think that while Thou dost suffer even to die of anguish upon this wood, there are yet so few souls that have the heart to love Thee! O my God! how many hearts are there at the present moment, even among those that are consecrated to Thee, who either love Thee not, or love Thee not enough! O beautiful flame of love, thou that didst consume the life of a God upon the cross, oh, consume me too; consume all the disorderly affections which live in my heart, and make me live burning and sighing only for that loving Lord of mine, who, for love of me, was willing to end his life, consumed by torments, upon a gibbet of ignominy! O my beloved Jesus! I wish ever to love Thee, and Thee alone, alone; my only wish is to love my love, my God, my all.

IV.

*Thine eyes shall behold thy teacher.*[1] It was promised to men that with their own eyes they should see their divine Master. The whole life of Jesus was one continuous example and school of perfection; but never did he better incalculate his own most excellent virtues than from the pulpit of his cross. There what an admirable instruction does he give us on patience, more especially in time of infirmity; for with what constancy does Jesus upon the cross endure with most perfect patience the pains of his most bitter death! There, by his own example, he teaches us an exact obedience to the divine precepts, a perfect

[1] *Isa.* xxx. 20.

resignation to God's will; and, above all, he teaches us how we ought to love. Father Paul Segneri, the younger, wrote to one of his penitents, that she ought to keep these words written at the foot of the crucifix: "See what it is to love." It seems as though our Redeemer from the cross said to us all, "See what it is to love," whenever, in order to avoid something that is troublesome, we abandon works that are pleasing in his sight, or at times even go so far as to renounce his grace and his love. He has loved us even unto death, and came not down from the cross till after having left his life thereon.

Ah, my Jesus, Thou hast loved me, even unto dying for me; and I too wish to love Thee even unto dying for Thee. How often have I offended and betrayed Thee in time past! O my Lord, revenge Thyself upon me; but let it be the revenge of pity and love. Bestow upon me such a sorrow for my sins as may make me live in continual grief and affliction through pain at having offended Thee. I protest my willingness to suffer every evil for the time to come, rather than displease Thee. And what greater evil could befall me than that of displeasing Thee, my God, my Redeemer, my hope, my treasure, my all.

V.

*And I, if I be lifted up from the earth, will draw all things to Myself. But this He said, signifying what death He should die.*[1] Jesus Christ said that when he should have been lifted up upon the cross, he would, by his merits, by his example, and by the power of his

[1] *John*, xii. 32.

love, have drawn towards himself the affection of all souls: "He drew all the nations of the world to his love, by the merit of his blood, by his example, and by his love." Such is the commentary of Cornelius à Lapide. Behold, O redeemed souls (as Holy Church exhorts us), behold your Redeemer upon that cross, where his whole form breathes love, and invites you to love him: his head bent downwards to give us the kiss of peace, his arms stretched out to embrace us, his heart open to love us: "His whole figure" (as St. Augustine says) "breathes love, and challenges us to love him in return: his head bent downwards to kiss us, his hands stretched out to embrace us, his bosom open to love us."

Ah, my beloved Jesus, how could my soul have been so dear in Thy sight, beholding, as Thou didst, the wrongs that Thou wouldst have to receive at my hands! Thou, in order to captivate my affections, wert willing to give me the extremest proofs of love. Come, ye scourges, ye thorns, nails, and cross, which tortured the sacred flesh of my Lord, come ye, and wound my heart; be ever reminding me that all the good that I have received, and all that I hope for, comes to me through the merits of his Passion. O Thou master of love, others teach by word of mouth, but Thou upon this bed of death dost teach by suffering; others teach from interested motives, Thou from affection, asking no recompense excepting my salvation. Save me, O my love, and let my salvation be the bestowal of the grace ever to love and please Thee; the love of Thee is my salvation.

VI.

While Jesus was dying upon the cross, the men who were around him never ceased to torment him with reproaches and insults. Some said to him: *He saved others, Himself He cannot save.*[1] Others: *If He be the King of Israel, let Him now come down from the cross.*[2] And Jesus, while these are outraging him, what is he doing upon the cross? He is, perhaps, praying the Eternal Father to punish them? No; he is praying him to pardon them: *Father, forgive them, for they know not what they do.*[3] Yes, says St. Thomas; to show forth the immense love which he had for men, the Redeemer asked pardon of God for his very crucifiers: "To show forth the abundance of his charity, he asked pardon for his persecutors." He asked it, and obtained it; for, when they had seen him dead, they repented of their sin: *They returned smiting their breasts.*[4]

Ah, my dear Saviour, behold me at Thy feet: I have been one of the most ungrateful of Thy persecutors; do Thou for me likewise pray Thy Father to pardon me. True, indeed, it is that the Jews and the executioners knew not what they were doing when they crucified Thee; but I well knew that, in sinning, I was offending a God who had been crucified, and had died for me. But Thy blood and Thy death have merited, even for me, the divine mercy. I cannot feel doubtful

[1] *Matt.* xxvii. 42.
[2] *Ibid.*
[3] *Luke,* xxiii. 34.
[4] *Luke,* xxiii. 48.

of being pardoned, after I see Thee die to obtain pardon for me. Ah, my sweet Redeemer, turn towards me one of those looks of love wherewith Thou didst look upon me, when dying for me upon the cross! Look upon me and pardon me all the ungratefulness which I have shown to Thy love. I repent, O my Jesus, of having despised Thee. I love Thee with all my heart; and, at the sight of Thy example, because I love Thee, I love all those likewise who have offended me. I wish them all possible good, and I purpose to serve them to the utmost of my power, for love of Thee, O my Lord, who hast been willing to die for me, who have so much offended Thee.

VII.

*Remember me,*[1] said the good thief to Thee, O my Jesus; and he had the consolation of hearing these words from Thee: *This day thou shalt be with me in paradise.*[2]

Be mindful of me, say I likewise unto Thee; be mindful, O Lord, that I am one of those sheep for whom Thou didst give Thy life. Give me, too, the consolation of making me feel that Thou dost forgive me, vouchsafing me a great sorrow for my sins. Do Thou, O great priest, who dost sacrifice Thyself for love of Thy creatures, have compassion upon me. From this day forth do I sacrifice to Thee my will, my senses, my satisfactions, and all my desires. I believe that Thou, my God, didst die, crucified, for me. Let Thy divine blood, I pray Thee, flow also upon me; let it

---

1 *Luke,* xxiii. 42.
2 Ibid. 43.

wash me from my sins. Let it inflame me with holy love, and make me all Thine own. I love Thee, O my Jesus, and I wish that I could die, crucified, for Thee, who didst die, crucified, for me.

O Eternal Father, I have offended Thee; but behold Thy Son, who, hanging upon this tree, makes satisfaction to Thee for me with the sacrifice which he offers Thee of his divine life. I offer Thee his merits, which are all mine, for he has made them over to me; and, for love of this Thy Son, I pray Thee to have mercy upon me. The greatest mercy that I ask of Thee is, that Thou wouldst give me Thy grace, which, miserable wretch that I am, I have so often wilfully despised. I repent of having outraged Thee, and I love Thee, I love Thee, my God, my all; and, to please Thee, I am ready to endure every shame, every pain, every sorrow, and every death.

# CHAPTER XIII.

## THE LAST WORDS OF JESUS UPON HIS CROSS, AND HIS DEATH.

### I.

Jesus, by the mouth of the Prophet, made lamentation that, when dying upon the cross, he went in search of some one to console him, but found none: *And I looked for one that would comfort Me, and I found none.*[1] The Jews and the Romans, even while he was dying, uttered against him their execrations and blasphemies. The Most Holy Mary—yes, she stood beneath the cross, in order to afford him some relief, had it been in her power to do so; but this afflicted and loving Mother, by the sorrow which she suffered through sympathy with his pains, only added to the affliction of this her Son, who loved her so dearly. St. Bernard says that the pains of Mary all went towards increasing the torments of the Heart of Jesus: "The Mother being filled with it, the ocean of her sorrow poured itself back upon the Son." So that the Redeemer, in beholding Mary sorrowing thus, felt his soul pierced more by the sorrows of Mary than by his own; as was revealed to St. Bridget by the Blessed Virgin herself: "He, on beholding me, grieved more for me than for himself." Whence St. Bernard says, "O good Jesus, great as are Thy bodily sufferings, much more dost Thou suffer in Thy Heart

[1] *Ps.* lxviii. 21.

through compassion for Thy Mother." What pangs, too, must not those loving Hearts of Jesus and Mary have felt when the moment arrived in which the Son, before breathing his last, had to take his leave of the Mother! Behold what the last words were with which Jesus took his leave in this world of Mary: "Mother, behold Thy Son;" assigning to her John, whom, in his own place, he left her for a son.

O Queen of Sorrows, things given as memorials by a beloved son at the hour of his death, how very dear they are, and never do they slip away from the memory of a mother! Oh, bear it in mind that thy Son, who loved thee so dearly, has, in the person of John, left me, a sinner, to thee for a son. For the love which thou didst bear to Jesus, have compassion on me. I ask thee not the good things of earth; I behold thy Son dying in so great pains for me; I behold thee, my innocent Mother, enduring also for me so great sufferings; and I see that I, a miserable being, who deserve hell on account of my sins, have not suffered anything for love of thee—I wish to suffer something for thee before I die. This is the grace that I ask of thee; and, with St. Bonaventure, I say to thee: "O Lady, if I have offended thee, wound my heart for justice' sake; if I have served thee, I ask thee for wounds as my recompense." Obtain for me, O Mary, a great devotion and a continual remembrance of the Passion of thy Son; and, by that pang which Thou didst suffer on beholding him breathe his last upon the cross, obtain for me a good death. Come to my assistance, O my Queen, in that last moment; make me die, loving and pronouncing the sacred names of Jesus and of Mary.

II.

Jesus, seeing that he found no one to console him upon this earth, raised his eyes and his Heart to his Father, craving relief from him. But the Eternal Father, beholding the Son clad in the garment of a sinner, replied, No, my Son, I cannot give Thee consolation, now that Thou art making satisfaction to my justice for all the sins of men; it is fitting that I too should abandon Thee to Thy pains, and let Thee die without solace. And then it was that our Saviour, crying out with a loud voice, said, My God, my God, and why hast Thou too abandoned Me? *Jesus cried out with a loud voice, saying, My God, My God, why hast Thou forsaken Me?* [1] In his explanation of this passage, the Blessed Denis, the Carthusian, says that Jesus uttered these words with a loud cry, to make all men understand the greatness of the pain and sorrow in which he died. And it was the will of the loving Redeemer, adds St. Cyprian, to die bereft of every consolation, to give proof to us of his love, and to draw to himself all our love: "He was left in dereliction, that he might show forth his love towards us, and might attract our love towards himself."

Ah, my beloved Jesus, Thou art in the wrong to make Thy lamentation, saying, My God, why hast Thou abandoned me? "Why," dost Thou say? And why, I will say to Thee, hast Thou been willing to

[1] *Matt.* xxvii. 46.

undertake to pay our penalty? Didst Thou not know that for our sins we had already deserved to be abandoned by God? With good reason, then, is it that Thy Father hath abandoned Thee, and leaves Thee to die in an ocean of sufferings and griefs. Ah, my Redeemer, Thy dereliction gives me both affliction and consolation: it is afflicting to me to see Thee die in such great pain; but it is consoling, in that it encourages me to hope that, by Thy merits, I shall not remain abandoned by the divine mercy, according as I should deserve, for having myself so often abandoned Thee in order to follow my own humors. Make me understand that, if to Thee it was so hard to be deprived, even for a brief interval, of the sensible presence of God, what my pain would be if I were to be deprived of God forever. Oh, by this dereliction of Thine, suffered with so much pain, forsake me not, O my Jesus, especially at the hour of my death! Then, when all shall have abandoned me, do not Thou abandon me, my Saviour. Ah, my Lord, who wert so left in desolation, be Thou my comfort in my desolations! Already do I understand that, if I shall love Thee without consolation, I shall content Thy heart the more. But Thou knowest my weakness; help me by Thy grace, and then grant me perseverance, patience, and resignation.

III.

Jesus, drawing nigh unto death, said, "*Sitio,*" I thirst. Tell me Lord, says Leo of Ostia, for what dost Thou thirst? Thou makest no mention of those immense pains which Thou dost suffer upon the cross;

but Thou complainest only of thirst: "Lord, what dost Thou thirst for? Thou art silent about the cross, and criest out about the thirst." "My thirst is for your salvation," is the reply which St. Augustine makes for him. O soul, says Jesus, this thirst of mine is nothing but the desire which I have for thy salvation. He, the loving Redeemer, with extremest ardor, desires our souls and therefore he panted to give himself wholly to us by his death. This was his thirst, wrote St. Laurence Justinian: "He thirsted for us, and desired to give himself to us." St. Basil of Seleucia says, moreover, that Jesus Christ, in saying that he thirsted, would give us to understand that he, for the love which he bore us, was dying with the desire of suffering for us even more than what he had suffered: "O that desire, greater than the Passion!"

O most lovely God! because Thou lovest us, Thou dost desire that we should desire Thee: "God thirsts to be thirsted for," as St. Gregory teaches us. Ah, my Lord, dost Thou thirst for me, a most vile worm as I am? and shall I not thirst for Thee, my infinite God? Oh, by the merits of this thirst endured upon the cross, give me a great thirst to love Thee, and to please Thee in all things. Thou hast promised to grant us whatever we seek from Thee: *Ask, and ye shall receive.*[1] I ask of Thee but this one gift—the gift of loving Thee. I am, indeed, unworthy of it; but in this has to be the glory of Thy blood,—the turning of a heart into a great lover of Thee, which has, at one time, so greatly despised Thee; to make a perfect

---

[1] *John*, xvi. 24.

flame of charity of a sinner who is altogether full of mire and of sins. Much more than this hast Thou done in dying for me. Would that I could love Thee, O Lord infinitely good, as much as Thou dost deserve! I love Thee, O Eternal God; I love Thee, O infinite loveliness. Make me ever to increase in Thy love; reiterating to Thee frequent acts of love, and studying to please Thee in everything, without intermission and without reserve. Make me, wretched and insignificant as I may be, make me at least to be all Thine own.

IV.

Our Jesus, now on the point of expiring, in dying accents said, *It is finished.*[1] He, while uttering the aforesaid word, ran over in his mind the whole course of his life. He beheld all the fatigues he had gone through,—the poverty, the pains, the ignominies he had suffered; and he offered them all anew to his Eternal Father for the salvation of the world. Then, turning himself back again to us, it seems as if he repeated, "It is finished;" as though he had said, O men, all is consummated; all is fulfilled; your redemption is accomplished; the divine justice is satisfied; Paradise is opened; *and behold your time, the time of lovers.*[2] It is time at last, O men, that you should surrender yourselves to my love. Love me, then; oh, love me; for there is nothing more that I can do in order to be loved by you. You see what I have done in order to gain your love. For you I have led a

---

[1] *John*, xix. 30.

[2] *Ezech.* xvi. 8.

life which has been but one series of tribulations. At its close, before I died, I have been content to let myself be drained of blood, have my face spit upon, my flesh torn to pieces, my head crowned with thorns; until I suffered the pains of agony upon this cross, as you see me now. What is there that remains? It only remains for me to die for you. Yes, it is my will to die. Come, O death; I give thee leave to take away my life for the salvation of my flock. And do you, my flock, love me, love me; for I can do no more in order to make myself beloved by you.

"It is consummated" (says the Blessed Tauler): "all that justice exacted, all that charity demanded, all that could have been done to give proof of love."

Oh, would that I too, my beloved Jesus, could say in dying, Lord, I have fulfilled all; I have accomplished all that Thou hast given me to do; I have borne my cross with patience; I have pleased Thee in all things. Ah, my God, were I now to die, I should not die content; for nothing of this could I say with truth. But am I always to live thus ungrateful to Thy love? Oh, grant me the grace to please Thee during the remainder of my life, that, when death shall come, I may be able to say to Thee, that from this time at least I have fulfilled Thy will. If in time past I have offended Thee, Thy death is my hope. For the future it is my wish not to betray Thee more; but from Thee it is that I hope for my perseverance. By Thy merits, O my Jesus, I ask and hope it from Thee.

V.

Behold Jesus, at length, actually dying. Behold him, my soul, how he is in his agony amid the last respirations of his life. Behold those dying eyes, that face so pale, that feebly palpitating heart, that body already wrapped in the arms of death, and that beautiful soul now on the point of leaving that wounded body. The sky shrouds itself in darkness; the earth quakes; the graves open. Alas, what portentous signs are these! They are signs that the Maker of the world is now dying.

Behold, in the last place, how our Redeemer, after having commended his blessed soul to his Eternal Father, first breathing forth from his afflicted Heart a deep sigh, and then bowing down his head in token of his obedience, and offering up his death for the salvation of men, at length, through the violence of the pain, expires, and delivers up his spirit into the hands of his beloved Father: *And crying out with a loud voice, He said, Father, into Thy hands I commend My Spirit; and saying this He gave up the ghost.*[1]

Draw near, O my soul, to the foot of that holy altar whereon the Lamb of God is now lying dead, sacrificed for thy salvation. Draw near, and reflect that he is dead for the love which he has borne thee. Ask your dead Lord for what you wish, and hope for all. O Saviour of the world, O my Jesus, behold to what Thy love for men has at length reduced Thee! I

[1] *Luke,* xxiii. 46.

thank Thee that Thou hast been willing, Thou, our God, to lose Thy life that we might not lose our souls. And who is there more than I that has reaped the fruits of Thy death? I, through Thy merits, without even so much as knowing it, was, in the outset, by baptism, made a child of the Church; through Thy love I have been forgiven so often since, and have received so many special graces; through Thee I have the hope of dying in the grace of God, and of coming to love Thee in Paradise.

O my beloved Redeemer, how greatly am I obliged to Thee! Into Thy pierced hands I commend my poor soul. Make me well understand what love there must have been in a God who died for me: would that I could, O Lord, die for Thee! But what would the death of a wicked slave weigh against the death of his Lord and God? Would that I could, at least, love Thee as much as I am able; but without Thy help, O my Jesus, I can do nothing. Oh, help me! and, through the merits of Thy death, make me die to all earthly affections, that so I may love Thee only, who dost deserve all my love. I love Thee, O infinite goodness, I love Thee, my chief good; and, with St. Francis, I pray Thee: "May I die for the love of Thy love, who didst vouchsafe to die for the love of my love." May I die to everything, out of gratitude, at least, for Thy great love, who hast vouchsafed to die, through Thy love for me, and in order to be beloved by me. O Mary, my Mother, intercede for me. Amen.

## CHAPTER XIV.

### THE HOPE WHICH WE HAVE IN THE DEATH OF JESUS CHRIST.

I.

Jesus is the only hope of our salvation: *There is no salvation in any other but Him.*[1] I am the only door, says he; and he that shall enter in through me shall assuredly find life eternal: *I am the door; if any one enter by Me, he shall be saved.*[2] And what sinner would ever have been able to hope for pardon if Jesus had not, by his blood and by his death, made satisfaction to the divine justice for us? *He shall bear their iniquities.*[3] It is by this that the Apostle encourages us, saying, *If the blood of goats and of oxen sanctify such as are defiled to the cleansing of the flesh, how much more shall the Blood of Christ, who through the Holy Ghost, offered Himself up to God, cleanse our conscience from dead works to serve the living God!*[4] If the blood of goats and of bulls offered up in sacrifice removed from the Jews the outward defilements of the body, that so they could be admitted to the worship of the sanctuary, how much more shall the blood of Jesus Christ, who for love offered himself up as a

[1] *Acts*, iv. 12.
[2] *John*, x. 9.
[3] *Isa*. liii. 11.
[4] *Heb*. ix. 13.

satisfaction for us, remove the sins from our souls to enable us to serve our God Most High!

Our loving Redeemer, having come into the world for no other end but that of saving sinners, and beholding the sentence of condemnation already recorded against us for our sins, what was it that he did? He by his own death paid the penalty that was due to ourselves; and with his own blood cancelling the sentence of condemnation, in order that the divine justice might no more seek from us the satisfaction due, he nailed it to the same cross whereon he died: *Blotting out the handwriting of the decree that was against us, which was contrary to us. And the same he took out of the way, fastening it to the cross.*[1] *Christ entered once into the holy place, having found for us eternal redemption.*[2]

Ah, my Jesus, hadst Thou not found this mode of obtaining pardon for us, who would ever have been able to find it? It was with reason that David cried out, *Declare His ways.*[3] Make known, O ye blessed, the loving contrivances which our God has employed in order to save us. Since, then, O my sweet Saviour, Thou hast had such a love for me, cease not from exercising mercy towards me. Thou, by Thy death, hast rescued me from the hands of Lucifer: into Thy hands do I consign my soul; it is for Thee to save it: *Into Thy hands I commend my spirit; Thou hast redeemed me, O God of truth.*[4]

---

[1] *Col.* ii. 14.
[2] *Heb.* ix. 12.
[3] *Ps.* ix. 12.
[4] *Ps.* xxx. 6.

II.

*Little children, these things I write to you, that you may not sin: but if any man sin, we have an Advocate with the Father, Jesus Christ the Just, and He is the propitiation for our sins.*[1] Jesus Christ did not, with his death, bring to an end his intercession for us with the Eternal Father: even at the present moment he is acting as our advocate; and it seems as if he knew not what else to do in heaven, as St. Paul writes, but be moving the Father to exercise mercy towards us: *ever living to make intercession for us.*[2] And the Apostle adds that this is the end for which our Saviour is ascended into heaven: *that He may now appear in the presence of God for us.*[3] As rebels are driven away from the presence of their king, so should we sinners have nevermore been deemed worthy of admission into the presence of our God, even so much as to ask his pardon; but Jesus, as our Redeemer, makes appearance for us in the divine presence, and, through his merits, obtains for us the grace that we had lost.

*You are come to Jesus the Mediator, and to the sprinkling of blood, which speaketh better than Abel.*[4] Oh, with how much greater effect does the blood of the Redeemer implore for us the divine mercy than did the blood of Abel plead for chastisement on Cain! My justice (said God to St. Mary Magdalen of Pazzi) is transformed into mercy by the vengeance taken on

[1] 1 *John*, ii. 1.
[2] *Heb.* vii. 25.
[3] *Heb.* ix. 24.
[4] *Heb.* xii. 22, 24.

the innocent flesh of Jesus Christ. The blood of this my Son pleads not with me for vengeance, like the blood of Abel, but pleads only for mercy and pity; and at the sound of this voice my justice cannot but rest appeased. This blood so binds its hands, that, so to speak, it cannot stir to take that vengeance upon sins which it used to take before.

*Be not unmindful of the kindness of thy Surety.*[1] Ah, my Jesus, I was already incapable, after my sins, of making satisfaction to the divine justice, when Thou, by Thy death, wert willing to make satisfaction for me. Oh, what ingratitude would mine be now, were I to be unmindful of this Thy so great mercy! No, my Redeemer, never will I be unmindful of it; I desire to be ever thanking Thee for it, and to show forth my thankfulness by loving Thee, and doing all that I can to please Thee. Do Thou aid me by that grace which Thou hast, by so many sufferings, merited for me. I love Thee, my Jesus, my love, my hope!

III.

*Come, O my dove, into the clefts of the rock.*[2] Oh, what a safe place of refuge shall we ever find in the sacred clefts of the rock, in the wounds, that is to say, of Jesus Christ! "The clefts of the rock," says St. Peter Damian, "are the Redeemer's wounds; in these has our soul placed its hope." There shall we be set free from that feeling of distrust which the sight of the sins that we have committed may produce; there shall we find weapons wherewith to defend ourselves

---

[1] *Ecclus.* xxix. 19.

[2] *Cant.* ii. 14.

when we shall be tempted to sin anew: *Have confidence, my children; I have overcome the world.*[1] If you have not sufficient strength (our Saviour exhorts us) to resist the assaults of the world, that offers you its pleasures, place your confidence in me, for I have overcome it; and thus shall you likewise overcome. Pray the Eternal Father, said he, for the sake of my merits, to give you strength, and I promise you that he will grant you whatever you ask of him in my name: *Amen, amen, I say unto you, if you ask anything of the Father in My name, He will give it you.*[2] And elsewhere he confirms to us the promise, saying that whatsoever grace we shall, for his love, ask of God, he himself, who is one with the Father, will give it us: *Whatsoever you shall ask of the Father in My name, that I will do: that the Father may be glorified in the Son.*[3]

Ah, Father Eternal, trusting to the merits and to these promises of Jesus Christ, I ask not of Thee the good things of earth, but Thy grace alone. True it is that, after the wrongs I have done Thee, I should not deserve either pardon or grace; yet, if I deserve them not, Thy Son hath merited them for me, by offering up his blood and his life for me. For the love, then, of this Thy Son, grant me Thy pardon. Give me a great sorrow for my sins, and a great love towards Thee. Enlighten me to know how lovely is Thy goodness, and how great is the love which Thou hast borne me from all eternity. Make known to me Thy will, and

---

[1] *John*, xvi. 33.
[2] *John*, xvi. 23.
[3] *Ibid.* xiv. 13.

give me strength to fulfil it perfectly. O Lord, I love Thee, and desire to do all that Thou dost desire of me.

IV.

Oh, how great is the hope of salvation which the death of Jesus Christ imparts to us: *Who is He that shall condemn? Christ Jesus who died, who also maketh intercession for us.*[1] Who is it, asks the Apostle, that has to condemn us? It is that same Redeemer who, in order not to condemn us to eternal death, condemned himself to a cruel death upon a cross. From this St. Thomas of Villanova encourages us, saying, What dost thou fear, sinner, if thou art willing to leave off thy sin? How should that Lord condemn thee, who died in order not to condemn thee? How should he drive thee away when thou returnest to his feet, he who came from heaven to seek thee when thou wert fleeing from him? "What art thou afraid of, sinner? How shall he condemn thee penitent, who dies that thou mayst not be condemned? How shall he cast thee off returning, who came from heaven seeking thee?" But greater still is the encouragement given us by this same Saviour of ours, when, speaking by Isaias, he says, *Behold, I have graven thee upon My hands; thy walls are always before My eyes.*[2] Be not distrustful, my sheep; see how much thou didst cost me. I keep thee engraven upon my hands, in these wounds which I have suffered for thee; these are ever reminding me to help

[1] *Rom.* viii. 34.

[2] *Isa.* xlix. 16.

thee, and to defend thee from thine enemies: love me and have confidence.

Yes, my Jesus, I love Thee, and feel confidence in Thee. To rescue me, yea, this has cost Thee dear; to save me will cost Thee nothing. It is Thy will that all should be saved, and that none should perish. If my sins cause me to dread, Thy goodness reassures me, more desirous as Thou art to do me good than I am to receive it. Ah, my beloved Redeemer, I will say to Thee with Job: *Even though Thou shouldst kill me, yet I will hope in Thee, and Thou wilt be my Saviour.*[1] Wert Thou even to drive me away from Thy presence, O my love, yet would not I leave off from hoping in Thee, who art my Saviour. Too much do these wounds of Thine and this blood encourage me to hope for every good from Thy mercy. I love Thee, O dear Jesus; I love Thee, and I hope.

V.

The glorious St. Bernard one day, in sickness, saw himself before the judgment-seat of God, where the devil was accusing him of his sins, and telling him that he did not deserve paradise: "It is true that I deserve not paradise," the saint replied; "but Jesus has a twofold title to this kingdom,—in the first place, as being by nature Son of God; in the next place, as having purchased it by his death. He contents himself with the first of these, and the second he makes over to me; and therefore it is that I ask and hope for paradise."

---

[1] *Job*, xiii. 15.

We, too, can say the same; for St. Paul tells us that the will of Jesus Christ to die, consumed by sufferings, had for its end the obtaining of paradise for all sinners that are penitent, and resolved to amend: *And, being perfected, He was made the cause of eternal salvation to all that obey Him.*[1] And hence the Apostle subjoins: *Let us run to the fight proposed unto us, looking on Jesus, the Author and Finisher of faith, who, having joy proposed unto Him, underwent the cross, despising the shame.*[2] Let us go forth with courage to fight against our enemies, fixing our eyes on Jesus Christ, who, together with the merits of his Passion, offers us the victory and the crown. He has told us that he is gone to heaven to prepare a place for us: *Let not your heart be trouble . . . ; for I go to prepare a place for you.*[3] He has told, and is continually telling, his Father that, since he has consigned us to him, he wishes us to be with him in paradise: *Father, those whom Thou hast given Me, I will that where I am they also may be with Me.*[4] "And what greater mercy could we have hoped for from the Lord, says St. Anselm, than for the Eternal Father to have said to a sinner, already for crimes condemned to hell, and with no means of delivering himself from its punishments, Take thou my Son, and offer him in thy stead?" And for the same Son to have said, Take me, and deliver thyself from hell? "What greater mercy can we imagine than that to one who, being a sinner,

---

[1] *Heb.* v. 9.
[2] *Heb.* xii. 1.
[3] *John*, xiv. 1-2.
[4] *John*, xvii. 24.

cannot redeem himself, God the Father should say, Accept of my only-begotten Son, and deliver him over to be punished in thy stead; and that the Son should say, Take me and redeem thyself? "

Ah, my loving Father, I thank Thee for having given me this Thy Son for my Saviour; I offer to Thee his death; and, for the sake of his merits, I pray Thee for mercy. And ever do I return thanks to Thee, O my Redeemer, for having given Thy blood and Thy life to deliver me from eternal death. "We pray Thee, therefore, help Thy servants, whom Thou hast redeemed with Thy precious blood." Help, then, us, Thy rebellious servants, since Thou hast redeemed us at so great a cost. O Jesus, my one and only hope! Thou dost love me. Thou hast power to do all things: make me a saint. If I am weak, do Thou give me strength; if I am sick, in consequence of the sins I have committed, do Thou apply to my soul one drop of Thy blood, and heal me. Give me the love of Thee, and final perseverance, making me die in Thy grace. Give me paradise; through Thy merits do I ask it of Thee, and hope to obtain it. I love Thee, O my most lovely God, with all my soul; and I hope to love Thee always. Oh, help a miserable sinner, who is wishing to love Thee.

VI.

*Having, therefore, a great High Priest, who hath penetrated the heavens, Jesus the Son of God, let us hold fast our confession. For we have not a high-priest who cannot have compassion on our infirmities, but one tempted in all things like as we are, yet without sin.*[1] Since, says the Apostle, we have this Saviour, who has opened to us paradise, which was at one time closed to us by sin, let us always have confidence in his merits; because, from having of his goodness willed to suffer in himself also our miseries, he well knows how to compassionate us: *Let us, therefore, go with confidence to the throne of grace, that we may obtain mercy, and find grace in seasonable aid.*[2] Let us, then, go with confidence to the throne of the divine mercy, to which we have access by means of Jesus Christ, that so we may there find all the graces that we need. And how can we doubt, subjoins St. Paul, but that God, having given us his Son, has given us together with that Son all his goods: *He delivered Him up for us all; how hath He not, with Him, given us all things?*[3] Cardinal Hugo comments on this: "He will give the lesser, that is to say eternal life, who hath given the greater, that is to say his own Son." That Lord will not deny us the lesser, which is eternal life, who has gone so far as to give us the greater, which is his own Son himself.

O my chief and only good! what shall I render Thee, miserable as I am, in return for so great a gift as that which Thou hast given me of Thy Son? To Thee will I, with David, say, *The Lord shall repay for me.*[4] Lord, I have not where with to recompense Thee. That same Son of Thine can alone render Thee worthy thanks; let him thank Thee in my stead. O

---

[1] *Heb.* iv. 14.
[2] *Heb.* iv. 14.
[3] *Rom.* viii. 32.
[4] *Ps.* cxxxvii. 8.

my most merciful Father! by the wounds of Jesus, I pray Thee to save me. I love Thee, O infinite goodness; and because I love Thee, I repent of having offended Thee. My God, my God, I wish to be all Thine own; accept of me for the sake of the love of Jesus Christ. Ah, my sweet Creator, is it possible that Thou, after having given me Thy Son, shouldst deny me the good things that belong to Thee,—Thy grace, Thy love, Thy paradise?

VII.

St. Leo declares that Jesus Christ, by his death, has brought us more good than the devil brought us evil in the sin of Adam: "We have gained greater things through the grace of Christ than we had lost through the envy of the devil." And this the Apostle distinctly says, when writing to the Romans: *Not as the offence so also is the gift. Where the offence abounded, grace did super abound.*[1] Cardinal Hugo explains it: "The grace of Christ is of greater efficacy than is the offence." There is no comparison, says the Apostle, between the sins of man and the gift which God has made us in giving us Jesus Christ; great as was the sin of Adam, much greater by far was the grace which Jesus Christ, by his Passion, merited for us: *I have come that they may have life, and that they may have it more abundantly.*[2] I am come into the world, the Saviour protests, to the end that mankind, who were dead through sin, may receive through me not only the life of grace, but a life yet more abundant

[1] *Rom.* v. 15-20.
[2] *John,* x. 10.

than that which they had lost by sin. Wherefore it is that Holy Church calls the sin happy which has merited to have such a Redeemer: "O happy fault, which deserved such and so great a Redeemer."

*Behold, God is my Saviour, I will deal confidently, and will not fear.*[1] If, then, O my Jesus, Thou, who art an omnipotent God, art also my Saviour, what fear shall I have of being damned? If, in time past, I have offended Thee, I repent of it with all my heart. From this time forth I wish to serve Thee, to obey Thee, and to love Thee. I firmly hope that Thou, my Redeemer, who hast done and suffered so much for my salvation, wilt not deny me any grace that I shall need in order to be saved: "I will act with confidence, firmly hoping that nothing necessary to salvation will be denied me by Him who has done and suffered so much for my salvation."

VIII.

*You shall draw water from the fountains of the Saviour, and you shall say in that day, Praise ye the Lord, and call upon His name.*[2] The wounds of Jesus Christ are now the blessed fountains from which we can draw forth all graces, if we pray unto him with faith: *And a fountain shall come forth from the house of the Lord, and shall water the torrent of thorns.*[3] The death of Jesus, says Isaias, is precisely this promised fountain, which has bathed our souls in the water of grace, and, from being thorns of sins, has,

---

[1] *Isa.* xii. 2.
[2] *Isa.* xii. 3.
[3] *Joel,* iii. 8.

by his merits, transformed them into flowers and fruits of life eternal. He, the loving Redeemer, made himself, as St. Paul tells us, poor in this world, in order that we, through the merit of his poverty, might become rich: *For your sakes He became poor, that, through His poverty, you might be rich.*[1] By reason of sin we were ignorant, unjust, wicked, slaves of hell; but Jesus Christ, says the Apostle, by dying and making satisfaction for us, *is by God made for us Wisdom, Justice, Sanctification, and Redemption.*[2] That is to say, as St. Bernard explains it, "Wisdom, in his preaching, justice in his absolving, sanctification in his conduct, redemption in his Passion." He has made himself our wisdom by instructing us, our justice by pardoning us, our sanctity by his example, and our redemption by his Passion, delivering us from the hands of Lucifer. In short, as St. Paul says, the merits of Jesus Christ have enriched us with all good things, so that we no more want for anything in order to be able to receive all graces: *In all things you are made rich; so that nothing is wanting to you in any grace.*[3]

O my Jesus, my Jesus, what beautiful hopes does Thy Passion give me! O my beloved Saviour, how much do I owe Thee! Oh, would that I had never offended Thee! Oh, pardon me all the wrongs that I have done Thee; inflame me fully with Thy love, and save me in eternity. And how can I be afraid of not receiving forgiveness, salvation, and every grace,

---

[1] 2 *Cor.* viii. 9.
[2] 1 *Cor.* i. 30.
[3] 1 *Cor.* i. 5.

from an omnipotent God who has given me all his blood? Ah, my Jesus, my hope, Thou, in order not to lose me, hast been willing to lose Thy life; I will not lose Thee, O infinite good. If, in time past, I have lost Thee, I repent of it; I wish, for the future, never to lose Thee more. It is for Thee to aid me, that I may not lose Thee again. O Lord, I love Thee, and I will love Thee always. Mary, thou, next after Jesus, art my hope; tell thy Son that thou dost protect me, and I shall be safe. Amen. So may it be.

# CHAPTER XV.

## THE LOVE OF THE ETERNAL FATHER IN HAVING GIVEN US HIS SON.

### I.

*God so loved the world, that He gave His only-begotten Son.*[1] God, says Jesus Christ, has loved the world to that degree that he has given it his own and only Son. In this gift there are three things demanding our consideration: Who is the giver, what is the thing given, and the greatness of the love wherewith he gives it? We are already aware that the more exalted the donor is, the more to be prized is the gift. One who receives a flower from a monarch will set a higher value on that flower than on a large amount of money. How much ought we not, then, to prize this gift, coming to us, as it does, from the hands of one who is God! And what is it that he has given us? His own Son. The love of this God did not content itself with having given us so many good things on this earth, until it had reached the point of giving us its whole self in the person of the Incarnate Word: "He gave us not a servant, not an Angel, but his own Son," says St. John Chrysostom. Wherefore Holy Church exultingly exclaims, "O wondrous condescension of Thy mercy in our regard! O unappreciable

[1] *John*, iii. 16.

love of charity! that Thou mightest redeem a slave, Thou deliveredst up Thy Son."

O infinite God, how couldst Thou condescend to exercise towards us so wondrous a compassion! Who shall ever be able to understand an excess so great as that, in order to ransom the slave, Thou wert willing to give us Thine only Son? Ah, my kindest Lord, since Thou hast given me the best that Thou hast, it is but just that I should give Thee the most that I can. Thou desirest of me my love: of Thee I desire nothing else, but only Thy love. Behold this miserable heart of mine; I consecrate it wholly to Thy love. Depart from my heart, all ye creatures; give room to my God, who deserves and desires to possess it wholly, and without companions. I love Thee, O God of love; I love Thee above everything: and I desire to love Thee alone, my Creator, my treasure, my all.

II.

God hath given us his Son; and why? For love alone. Pilate, for fear of men, gave Jesus up to the Jews: *He delivered Him up to their will.*[1] But the Eternal Father gave his Son to us for the love which he bore us: *He delivered Him up for us all.*[2] St. Thomas says that "love has the nature of a first gift." When a present is made us, the first gift that we receive is that of the love which the donor offers us in the thing that he gives: because, observes the Angelic Doctor, the one and only reason of every voluntary gift is love; otherwise, when a gift is made for some

[1] *Luke,* xxiii. 25.
[2] *Rom.* viii. 32.

other end than that of simple affection, the gift can no longer rightly be called a true gift. The gift which the Eternal Father made us of his Son was a true gift, perfectly voluntary, and without any merit of ours; and therefore it is said that the Incarnation of the Word was effected through the operation of the Holy Spirit: that is, through love alone; as the same holy Doctor says: "Through God's supreme love it was brought to pass, that the Son of God assumed to himself flesh."

But not only was it out of pure love that God gave unto this his Son, he also gave him to us with an immensity of love. This is precisely what Jesus wished to signify when he said: *God so loved the world.*[1] The word "so" (says St. John Chrysostom) signifies the magnitude of the love wherewith God made us this great gift: "The word 'so' signifies the vehemence of the love." And what greater love could one who was God have been able to give us than was shown by his condemning to death his innocent Son in order to save us miserable sinners? *Who spared not His own Son, but delivered Him up for us all.*[2] Had the Eternal Father been capable of suffering pain, what pain would he not, have then experienced, when he saw himself compelled by his justice to condemn that Son, whom he loved with the same love wherewith he loved himself, to die by so cruel a death in the midst of so many ignominies? *And the Lord willed to bruise*

---

[1] *John*, iii. 16.

[2] *Rom.* viii. 32.

*Him in infirmity.*[1] He willed to make him die consumed by torments and sufferings.

Imagine thyself, then, to behold the Eternal Father, with Jesus dead in his arms, and saying to us: This, O men, is my beloved Son, in whom I have found all my delights: *This is My beloved Son in whom I am well pleased.*[2] Behold how I have willed to see him ill-treated on account of your iniquities: *For the wickedness of My people have I smitten Him.*[3] Behold how I have condemned him to die upon this cross, afflicted, and abandoned even by myself, who love him so much. This have I done in order that you may love me.

O infinite goodness! O infinite mercy! O infinite love! O God of my soul! since Thou didst will that the object most dear to Thy heart should die for me, I offer to Thee in my own behalf that great sacrifice of himself which this Thy Son made Thee; and for the sake of his merits, I pray Thee to give me the pardon of my sins, Thy love, and Thy paradise. Great as are these graces which I ask of Thee, the offering which I present unto Thee is greater still. For the love of Jesus Christ, O my Father, pardon me and save me. If I have offended Thee in time past, I repent of it above every evil. I now prize Thee, and love Thee, above every good.

---

[1] *Isa.* liii. 10.

[2] *Matt.* iii. 17.

[3] *Isa.* liii. 8.

III.

Ah, who but a God of infinite love could ever have loved us to such a degree? St. Paul writes: *But God, who is rich in mercy, on account of the too great love wherewith He loved us when we were dead in sins, quickened us together in Christ.*[1] The Apostle calls too great this love which God showed us in giving to men, by means of the death of his Son, the life of grace which they had lost by their sins. But to God, who is love itself, this love was not too great: *God is love.*[2] St. John says that herein he wished to make us see the extent to which the greatness of the love of a God towards us reached, in sending his own Son into the world to obtain for us, by his death, forgiveness and life eternal: *By this hath appeared the charity of God in us, because God hath sent His own only-begotten Son into the world, that we might have life through Him.*[3]

By sin, we were dead to the life of grace; and Jesus, by his death, has brought us back to life. We were miserable, deformed objects of abomination; but God, by means of Jesus Christ, has rendered us pleasing and precious in his divine sight. *He hath made us* (wrote the apostle) *acceptable through His beloved Son.*[4] He hath made us acceptable, i.e., "He hath made us pleasing," says the Greek text. And therefore St. John Chrysostom adds that were there

---

1 *Ephes.* ii. 4.

2 1 *John,* iv. 16.

3 1 *John,* iv. 9.

4 *Ephes.* i. 6.

to be a poor leper all covered with wounds and disfigurements, and any one were to heal his body of the leprosy, and make him beautiful and rich besides, how great would be the sense of obligation that he would retain towards this his benefactor! How much more, then, are we now beholden to God, since, when our souls were disfigured and hateful on account of our sins, he hath, by means of Jesus Christ, not only delivered us from our sins, but has made them beautiful and lovely besides: *He hath blessed us with all spiritual blessings in heavenly places in Christ.*[1] Cornelius à Lapide comments upon this: "He hath bestowed upon us every spiritual gift." God's blessing involves benefaction. The Eternal Father, then, in giving us Jesus Christ, hath loaded us with all gifts, not indeed earthly ones in the body, but spiritual ones in the soul: *In heavenly places;*[2] giving us, together with his Son, a heavenly life in this world, and a heavenly glory in the other.

Give me, then, Thy blessings and Thy benefactions, O my most loving God, and may the benediction draw me wholly to Thy love: "Draw me by the chains of Thy love," Let the love which Thou hast borne me make me enamoured of Thy goodness. Thou dost deserve an infinite love; I love Thee with all the love I can command; I love Thee above everything; I love Thee more than myself. I give Thee my whole will; and this is the grace that I ask of Thee: make me from this day forth to live and do

[1] *Ibid.* 3.
[2] *Ibid.* 3.

everything according to Thy divine will, wherewith Thou desirest nothing but my good, and my eternal salvation.

IV.

*The King hath brought me into the cellar of wine; He hath set in order charity in me.*[1] My Lord, said the holy spouse, hath taken me into the cellar of wine; that is to say, hath placed before mine eyes all the benefits that he hath done me in order that I may be induced to love him: *He hath set in order charity in me.* A certain writer says that God, in order to gain our love, has, so to say, despatched against us an army of the graces of love. "He drew up charity against me like an armed host." But, says Cardinal Hugo, the gift of Jesus Christ to us was the reserved arrow of which Isaias prophesied: *He hath made me as a chosen arrow: in his quiver He hath hidden me.*[2] As the hunter, says Hugo, keeps the best arrow in reserve to give the finishing stroke to his game, so did God, amongst all his other benefits, keep Jesus in reserve, until the time of grace had arrived, and then he sent him forth, as if to give the finishing stroke of love to the hearts of men: "The chosen arrow is kept in reserve: so was Christ kept in reserve in the bosom of the Father, until the fulness of time should come; and then he was sent forth to wound the hearts of the faithful." St. Peter, wounded by this

---

[1] *Cant.* ii. 4.

[2] *Isa.* xlix. 2.

arrow, says St John Chrysostom, said to his Master: *Lord, Thou knowest that I love Thee.*[1]

Ah, my God, I behold myself surrounded on all sides with the artifices of Thy love. I do, likewise, love Thee; and if I love Thee, I know that Thou too dost love me. And what power shall ever deprive me of Thy love? Sin only. But from this infernal monster it is for Thee, through Thy mercy, to deliver me. I am content to suffer every evil, the most cruel death, or even to be torn to pieces, sooner than offend Thee by mortal sin. But Thou already knowest my past falls; Thou knowest my weakness; help me, O my God, for love of Jesus Christ: *Despise not Thou the work of Thine hands*,[2] I am the workmanship of Thy hands; Thou hast created me; despise me not. If I merit to be left to myself by reason of my sins, I merit nevertheless that Thou be merciful towards me for love of Jesus Christ, who hath sacrificed his life to Thee for my salvation. I offer up to Thee his merits, which all are mine; and, through them, I ask of Thee, and hope for, from Thee, the gift of holy perseverance, together with a good death; and meanwhile to live the remainder of my life entirely to Thy glory. Long enough have I offended Thee! I now repent of it with all my heart, and I wish to love Thee to the uttermost of my power. I desire no longer to offer resistance to Thy love: I surrender myself wholly unto Thee. Give me Thy grace, and Thy love, and then do with me what Thou wilt. I love Thee, O my God, and I wish, and I ask of

---

[1] *John*, xxi. 15.

[2] *Ps.* cxxxvii. 8.

Thee, to love Thee always. Oh, for the merits of Jesus Christ, hearken unto my prayer. Mary, my Mother, pray to God for me. Amen. So may it be.

# CHAPTER XVI.

## THE LOVE OF THE SON OF GOD IN HAVING WILLED TO DIE FOR US.

### I.

*And behold Thy time was the time of lovers. . . . And Thou wast made exceeding beautiful.*[1] How deeply are we Christians indebted to the Lord, in that he has caused us to be born after the coming of Jesus Christ! Our time is no longer a time of fear, as was that of the Jews, but a time of love; having seen a God dead for our salvation, and in order to gain our love. It is of faith that Jesus has loved us, and for love of us has given himself over unto death: *Christ hath loved us, and hath delivered Himself up for us.*[2] And where would ever have been the power to make an omnipotent God die, had not he of himself voluntarily willed to give his life for us? *I give My life . . . no one taketh it from Me; but I lay it down of Myself.*[3] Wherefore St. John observes that Jesus, by his death, gave us the uttermost proof that he could have given us of his love: *Having loved His own, He loved them to the end.*[4] Jesus, by his death, says a devout writer, gave us the greatest possible sign of his love, beyond which there remained for him nothing that

[1] *Ezech.* xvi. 8, 13.
[2] *Ephes.* v. 2.
[3] *John,* x. 17.
[4] *John,* xiii. 1.

he could do in order to show how much he loved us: "The highest proof of love was that which he showed forth at the end of his life upon the cross."

O my beloved Redeemer, Thou hast for love given Thyself wholly unto me; for love I give myself wholly unto Thee. Thou for my salvation hast given Thy life; I for Thy glory wish to die, when and as Thou dost please. There was nothing more that Thou couldst do in order to gain my love; but I have ungratefully exchanged Thee away for nothing. I repent of it, O my Jesus, with all my heart. Pardon me through Thy Passion; and in token of pardon, help me to love Thee. Through Thy grace I feel within myself a great desire of loving Thee, and I resolve to be all Thine own; but I see my languidness and the betrayals of which I have been guilty. Thou alone canst help me and render me happy. Help me, then, O my love. Make me love Thee: I ask Thee for nothing more.

II.

The Blessed Denis, the Carthusian, says that the Passion of Jesus Christ was called an excess—*And they spake of His excess, which he would accomplish in Jerusalem*[1]—because it was an excess of mercy and of love: "The Passion of Jesus Christ is said to be an excess, because in it was shown forth an excess of love and of compassion." O my God, and where is the believer that could live without loving Jesus Christ, if he were frequently to meditate upon his Passion? The wounds of Jesus, says St. Bonaventure, are all of them wounds of love. They are darts and flames

[1] *Luke*, ix. 31.

which wound the hardest hearts, and kindle into a flame the most frozen souls: "O wounds that wound stony hearts, and set frozen minds on fire!" In order the more strongly to impress upon his heart a love towards Jesus in his Passion, the Blessed Henry Suso one day took a knife, and cut out in letters upon his breast the name of his beloved Lord. And when thus bathed in blood, he went into the church, and, prostrating himself before the crucifix, he said, Behold, O Lord, Thou only Love of my soul, behold my desire. I would gladly have written Thee deeper within my heart; but this I cannot do. Do Thou, who canst do all things, supply what is wanting in my powers, and imprint Thy adorable name in the lowest depths of my heart, that so it may no more be possible to cancel in it either Thy name or Thy love.

*My Beloved is white and ruddy, chosen out of thousands.*[1] O my Jesus, Thou art all white through Thy spotless innocence: but upon this cross Thou art also all ruddy with wounds suffered for me. I choose Thee for the one and only object of my love. And whom shall I love, if I love not Thee? What is there that I can find amongst all other objects more lovely than Thee, my Redeemer, my God, my all? I love Thee, O most lovely Lord. I love Thee above everything. Do Thou make me love Thee with all my affection, and without reserve.

III.

"Oh, if thou didst know the mystery of the cross," said St. Andrew to the tyrant. O tyrant (it was his

[1] *Cant.* v. 10.

wish to say), wert thou to understand the love which Jesus Christ has borne thee, in willing to die upon a cross to save thee, thou wouldst abandon all thy possessions and earthly hopes, in order to give thyself wholly to the love of this thy Saviour. The same ought to be said to those Catholics who, believing as they do, the Passion of Jesus, yet do not think of it. Ah, were all men to think upon the love which Jesus Christ has shown forth for us in his death, who would ever be able not to love him? It was for this end, says the Apostle, that he, our beloved Redeemer, died for us, that, by the love he displayed towards us in his death, he might become the possessor of our hearts: *To this end Christ died, and rose again, that he might be Lord both of the dead and of the living; therefore, whether we live, or whether we die, we are the Lord's.* Whether, then, we die or live, it is but just that we belong wholly to Jesus, who has saved us at so great a cost.

O my dear Lord! Thou didst die in order to gain my soul; but what have I done in order to gain Thee, O infinite good? Ah, my Jesus, how often have I lost Thee for nothing! Miserable that I was, I knew at the time that I was losing Thy grace by my sin; I knew that I was giving Thee great displeasure; and yet I committed it. My consolation is, that I have to deal with an infinite goodness, who remembers his offences no more when a sinner repents and loves him. Yes, my God, I do repent and love Thee. Oh, pardon me; and do Thou from this day forth bear rule in this rebellious heart of mine. To Thee do I consign it; to Thee do I wholly give myself. Tell me what Thou dost desire; wishing, as I do, to perform it all. Yes, my Lord, I wish to love Thee; I wish to please Thee in everything. Do Thou give me strength, and I hope to do so.

IV.

Jesus has not, by dying, ceased to love us. He loves us, and seeks us with the self-same love wherewith he first of all came down from heaven to seek us and to die for us. That artifice of love, too, which was manifested by our Redeemer to St. Francis Xavier, while on his travels, is celebrated far and wide. In a storm at sea there came a wave which carried away from him his crucifix. As the saint, after landing, was standing upon the shore, sorrowing, and earnestly longing to recover, if he might, the image of his beloved Lord, behold he saw a crab coming towards him, holding up the crucifix between its claws. Then, going forward to meet it with tears of tenderness and love, he received it, and clasped it to his bosom.

Oh, with what love does Jesus go to that soul that seeks him—*The Lord is good . . . to the soul that seeketh Him*[1]—to the soul that seeketh him, however, with true love! But can they think that they possess this true love who refuse the crosses which the Lord sends them? *Christ pleased not Himself.*[2] "Christ," (as Cornelius à Lapide explains this passage) "served not his own will and convenience; but all this and his life itself did he expose for our salvation." Jesus, for love of us, sought not earthly pleasures; but he

[1] *Lam.* iii. 25.
[2] *Rom.* xv. 3.

sought sufferings and death, all innocent though he was; yet what is there that we are seeking for love of Jesus Christ? St. Peter the Martyr was one day standing in his prison, complaining of an unjust accusation which had been preferred against him, saying, "But, Lord, what have I done that I should have had to suffer this persecution?" When the crucifix made him this reply, "And I, what evil have I done that I should have had to be upon this cross?"

O my dear Saviour, Thou didst say, what evil hast Thou done? Too much hast Thou loved us; since for love of us Thou hast been willing to suffer so much. And shall we, who deserved hell for our sins, refuse to suffer that which Thou dost will for our good? Thou, my Jesus, art all love with whomsoever seeketh Thee. It is not Thy sweetnesses and consolations that I seek; I seek only Thyself and Thy will. Give me Thy love, and then do with me whatsoever Thou dost please. I embrace all the crosses which Thou wilt send me—poverty, persecutions, sickness, and pain. Deliver me only from the evil of sin, and then lay upon me every other evil. All will be but little in comparison with the evils which Thou hast suffered for love of me.

V.

"That he might redeem a slave, the Father neither spared the Son, nor did the Son spare himself." To liberate the slave, then, the Father hath not pardoned the Son, neither hath the Son pardoned himself. And after so great a love to men, will it be possible for there to be one who loves not this God, so loving as he is? The Apostle says that Jesus died for us all, to the end that we might live only to him and to his love: *Christ died for ally that they who live may no longer live unto themselves, but unto Him who died for them.*[1] But, alas! the greater portion of mankind, although one who is God has died for them, live unto sin, unto the devil, and not unto Jesus Christ. It was said by Plato that "love is the magnet of love." And Seneca replied, Do thou love, if thou wouldst be beloved: " If you would be loved, love." And how does it happen that Jesus, who, by dying for men, would seem to have gone foolish, as it were, out of love for us—" It seemed foolish that the author of life should die for all," says St. Gregory—how does it happen that he, after so many tokens of love on his part, has not been able to draw to himself our hearts? How is it that, loving us so much, he has not yet been able to make himself beloved by us?

Oh that all men loved Thee, my most lovely Jesus! Thou art a God worthy of infinite love. But, my poor Lord,—give me leave so to call Thee,—Thou art so lovely, Thou hast done and suffered so much in order to be loved by men; and, after all, how many are they that do love Thee? I see almost all men applying themselves to the love—some of their parents, some of their friends, some of wealth, honors, or pleasures, and some even of dumb animals; but how many are they that love Thee, O infinite loveliness? O God, too few, indeed, they are; yet amongst these few I wish to be—I, miserable sinner as I am, who at one time

---

[1] 2 *Cor.* v. 15.

also offended Thee by loving that which is but mire, going astray from Thee. But now I love Thee, and I prize Thee above every good: and Thee only do I wish to love. Do Thou pardon me, O my Jesus, and come to my assistance.

VI.

God, then, O Christian, says St. Cyprian, rests content with thee, even to dying in order to gain thy love; and wilt not thou rest content with God, so that thou wilt love objects other than thy Lord? "God is content with thee, and wilt thou not be content with thy God?" Ah, no; my beloved Jesus, I will not have any love in me which is not for Thee. I am content with Thee; I renounce all other loves: Thy love alone is enough for me. I hear Thee saying to me, *Put Me as a seal upon thy heart.*[1] Yes, my crucified Jesus, I do set Thee, and do Thou, too, set Thyself, as a seal upon my heart, that it may remain closed against every other love which tends not to Thee. In time past I have given Thee displeasure by means of other loves; but, at the present moment, there is no pain that afflicts me excepting the remembrance of having, by my sins, lost my love of Thee. For the future, *Who shall separate me from the love of Christ?*[2] Who shall ever again separate me from my love for Thee?

No, my most lovely Saviour, since Thou hast made me know the love which Thou hast borne me, I have not the heart to live any more without loving Thee. I love Thee, my crucified Love; I love Thee with all my

---

[12] *Cant.* viii. 6.

[2] *Rom.* viii. 3..

heart; and I give unto Thee this soul of mine, which Thou hast so much sought and loved. Oh, by the merits of Thy death, which so painfully separated Thy blessed soul from Thy body, do Thou detach me from every love which can hinder me from being all Thine own, and from loving Thee with all my heart. Mary, my hope, do thou help me to love thy sweetest Son alone, that so I may be able with truth, throughout my whole life, ever to repeat, "My Love is crucified; my Love is crucified." Amen.

---

*Prayer of St. Bonaventure.*

O Jesus! who, for my sake, hast not pardoned Thyself, do Thou so impress upon me Thy Passion that, wheresoever I turn, I may behold Thy wounds, and find no repose but in Thee and in the contemplation of Thy sufferings. Amen.

# Darts of Fire;

## *OR PROOFS THAT JESUS CHRIST HAS GIVEN US OF HIS LOVE IN THE WORK OF REDEMPTION.* [1]

To any one who considers the immense love which Jesus Christ has shown us in his life, and especially in his death, it is impossible not to be stirred up and excited to love a God who is so enamoured of our souls. St. Bonaventure calls the wounds of our Redeemer wounds which pierce the hardest hearts, and inflame divine love in the coldest souls.

Therefore, in this short examination of the love of Jesus Christ, let us consider, according to the testimony of the divine Scriptures, how much our loving Redeemer has done to make us understand the love that he bears us, and to oblige us to love him.

---

[1] Saint Alphonsus set a high value on this little treatise. He recommends it in several places of his works, and we read in one of his spiritual letters (December 18, 1767) that he himself used it nearly every day. In it is to be found the expression of those sentiments with which the saintly author mostly loved to nourish himself, and by which he sanctified his soul. In this treatise are chiefly repeated, under every form, the most fervent acts of contrition and of love. "They are irresistible darts that pierce the hardest hearts, and inflame divine love in the coldest souls." These pious reflections may be especially used when we are in the presence of the Blessed Sacrament, in our Visits, before and after Holy Communion, during Holy Mass and other divine services, or when we meditate on the Passion of our Lord. This treatise, entitled *Darts of Fire*, was published by the holy author in 1767.

I.

*Dilexit nos, et tradidit semetipsum pro nobis.*

"He hath love us, and hath delivered Himself for us."—*Ephes. v. 2.*

God had conferred so many blessings on men, thereby to draw them to love him; but these ungrateful men not only did not love him, but they would not even acknowledge him as their Lord. Scarcely in one corner of the earth, in Judea, was he recognized as God by his chosen people; and by them he was more feared than loved. He, however, who wished to be more loved than feared by us, became man like us, chose a poor, suffering, and obscure life, and a painful and ignominious death; and why? to draw our hearts to himself. If Jesus Christ had not redeemed us, he would not have been less great or less happy than he has always been; but he determined to procure our salvation at the cost of many labors and sufferings, as if his happiness depended on ours. He might have redeemed us without suffering; but no, he willed to free us from eternal death by his own death; and though he was able to save us in a thousand ways, he chose the most humiliating and painful way of dying on the cross of pure suffering, to purchase the love of us, ungrateful worms of the earth. And what indeed was the cause of his miserable birth and his most sorrowful death, if not the love he had for us?

Ah, my Jesus, may that love which made Thee die for me on Calvary destroy in me all earthly affections, and consume me in the fire which Thou art come to kindle on the earth. I curse a thousand times those shameful passions which cost Thee so much pain. I repent, my dear Redeemer, with all my heart for all the offences I have committed against Thee. For the future I will rather die than offend Thee; and I wish to do all that I can to please Thee. Thou hast spared nothing for my love; neither will I spare anything for Thy love. Thou hast loved me without reserve; I also without reserve will love Thee. I love Thee, my only good, my love, my all.

II.

*Sic Deus dilexit mundum, ut Filium suum unigenitum daret.*

"God so loved the world, as to give His only-begotten Son."—*John*, iii. 16.

Oh, how much does that little word *so* mean! It means that we shall never be able to comprehend the extent of such a love as this which made a God send his Son to die, that lost man might be saved. And who would ever have been able to bestow on us this gift of infinite value but a God of infinite love?

I thank thee, O Eternal Father! for having given me Thy Son to be my Redeemer; and I thank Thee, O great Son of God, for having redeemed me with so much suffering and love. What would have become of me, after the many sins that I have committed against Thee, if Thou hadst not died for me? Ah, that I had died before I had offended Thee, my Saviour! Make me feel some of that detestation for my sins which Thou hadst while on earth and pardon me. But pardon is not sufficient for me, Thou dost merit my love; Thou hast loved me even to death, unto death will I also love Thee. I love Thee, O infinite goodness, with all my soul; I love Thee more than myself; in Thee alone will I place all my affections. Do thou help me; let me no longer live ungrateful to Thee, as I have done hitherto. Tell me what Thou wouldst have of me, for, by Thy grace, all, all will I do. Yes, my Jesus, I love Thee, my treasure, my life, my love, my all.

III.

*Neque per sanguinem hircorum aut vitulorum, sed per proprium sanguinem introivit semel in sancta, æterna redemptione inventa.*

"Neither by the blood of goats or of calves, but by His own blood, entered once into the Holies, having obtained eternal redemption."—*Heb.* ix. 12.

And of what worth would the blood of all goats or even of all men be, if they were sacrificed to obtain divine grace for us? It is only the blood of this Man-God which would merit for us pardon and eternal salvation. But if God himself had not devised this way to redeem us, as he did by dying to save us, who ever would have been able to think of it? His love alone designed it and executed it. Therefore holy Job did well to cry out to this God who loves man so much: *What is man, O Lord, that Thou dost so exalt him? why is Thy heart so intent upon loving him? what is man that Thou shouldst magnify him? or why dost Thou set Thy heart upon him?* [1] Ah, my Jesus, one heart is but little with which to love Thee; if I loved Thee even with the hearts of all men, it would be too little. What in gratitude, then, would it be if I were to divide my heart between Thee and creatures! No, my love, Thou wouldst have it all, and well dost Thou

[1] *Job*, vii. 17.

deserve it; I will give it all to Thee. If I do not know how to give it Thee as I ought, take it Thyself, and grant that I may be able to say to Thee with truth, *God of my heart.*[1] Ah, my Redeemer, by the merits of the abject and afflicted life that Thou hast willed to live for me, give me true humility, which will make me love contempt and an obscure life. May I lovingly embrace all infirmities, affronts, persecutions and interior sufferings, and all the crosses which may come to me from Thy hands. Let me love Thee, and then dispose of me as Thou wilt. O loving heart of my Jesus! make me love Thee by discovering to me the immense good that Thou art. Make me all Thine before I die. I love Thee, my Jesus, who art worthy to be loved. I love Thee with all my heart, I love Thee with all my soul.

## IV.

*Benignitas et humanitas apparuit Salvatoris nostri Dei.*

"The goodness and kindness of God our Saviour appeared."—*Titus*, iii. 4.

God has loved man from all eternity: *I have loved thee with an everlasting love.*[2] "But," says St. Bernard, "before the Incarnation of the Word the divine Power appeared in creating the world, and the divine Wisdom in governing it; but when the Son of God became man, then was made manifest the love which God had for men." And, in fact, after seeing Jesus Christ go through so afflicted a life and so painful a death, we should be offering him an insult if we doubted the great love which he bears us. Yes, he

[1] *Ps.* lxxii. 26.

[2] *Jer.* xxxi. 3.

does surely love us; and because he loves us, he wishes to be loved by us. *And Christ died for all, that they also who live may not now live to themselves, but for Him who died for them and rose again.*[1]

Ah, my Saviour, when shall I begin to understand the love which Thou hast had for me? Hitherto, instead of loving Thee, I have repaid Thee with offences and contempt of Thy graces, but since Thou art infinite in goodness I will not lose confidence. Thou hast promised to pardon him who repents; for Thy mercy's sake fulfil Thy promise to me. I have dishonored Thee by putting Thee aside to follow my own pleasures; but now I grieve for it from the bottom of my soul, and there is no sorrow that afflicts me more than the remembrance of having offended Thee, my Sovereign Good; pardon me and unite me entirely to Thee by an eternal bond of love, that I may not leave Thee any more, and that I may only live to love Thee and to obey Thee. Yes, my Jesus, for Thee alone will I live, Thee only will I love. Once I left Thee for creatures, now I leave all to give myself wholly to Thee. I love Thee, O God of my soul, I love Thee more than myself. O Mary, Mother of God, obtain for me the grace to be faithful to God till death.

---

[1] 2 *Cor.* v. 15.

V.

*In hoc apparuit charitas Dei in nobis, quoniam Filium suum unigenitum misit Deus in mundum, ut vivamus per eum.*

"By this hath the charity of God appeared toward us, because God hath sent His only-begotten Son into the world that we might live by Him."
—1 *John*, iv. 9.

All men were dead by sin, and they would have remained dead if the eternal Father had not sent his Son to restore them to life by his death. But how? what is this? A God to die for man! A God! And who is this man? "Who am I?" says St. Bonaventure. "O Lord, why hast Thou loved me so much?" But it is in this that the infinite love of God shines forth. *By this hath the charity of God appeared.*[1] The Holy Church exclaims on Holy Saturday, "O wonderful condescension of Thy mercy toward us! O inestimable affection of charity! that Thou mightest redeem a slave, Thou didst deliver up Thy Son." O immense compassion! O prodigy! O excess of the love of God? to deliver a servant and a sinner from the death that he deserves, his innocent Son is condemned to die.

Thou, then, O my God, hast done this that we might live by Jesus Christ: *that we might live by Him.*[2] Yes, indeed, it is but meet that we should live for him, who has given all his blood and his life for us. My dear Redeemer, in the presence of Thy wounds and of the cross on which I see Thee dead for me, I consecrate to Thee my life and my whole will. Ah, make me all Thine, for from this day forward I

[1] 1 *John*, iv. 9.
[2] *Ibid.*

seek and desire none but Thee. I love Thee, infinite Goodness; I love Thee, in finite Love; while I live may I always repeat, *My God, I love Thee, I love Thee*; let my last words in death be, *My God, I love Thee, I love Thee.*

VI.

*Per viscera misericordiæ Dei nostri, in quibus visitavit nos Oriens ex alto.*

"Through the bowels of the mercy of our God, in which the Orient from on high hath visited us."—*Luke*, i. 78.

Behold, the Son of God comes on earth to redeem us, and he comes stimulated alone by the bowels of his mercy. But, O God! if Thou hast compassion on lost man, is it not enough that Thou shouldst send an angel to redeem him? No, says the Eternal Word, I will come myself, that man may know how much I love him. St. Augustine writes: "For this reason chiefly did Jesus Christ come, that man should know how much God loves him." But, my Jesus, even now that Thou hast come, how many men are there who truly love Thee? Wretch that I am, Thou knowest how I have hitherto loved Thee; Thou knowest what contempt I have had for Thy love. Oh that I might die of grief for it! I repent, my dear Redeemer, of having so despised Thee. Ah, pardon me, and at the same time give me grace to love Thee. Let me no longer remain unmindful of that great affection which Thou hast borne me. I love Thee now, but I love Thee but little. Thou dost merit an infinite love. Grant me at least that I may love Thee with all my strength. Ah, my Saviour, my joy, my life, my all, whom should I love if I love not Thee, the infinite Good? I consecrate all my wishes to Thy will; at the sight of the sufferings Thou hast undergone for me, I offer myself to suffer as much as it shall please Thee. *Lead us not into temptation, but deliver us from evil.* Deliver me from sin, and then dispose of me as Thou wilt. I love Thee, infinite Good, and I am content to receive any punishment, even to be annihilated, rather than to live without loving Thee.

### VII.

*Et Verbum caro factum est.*

"And the Word was made flesh."—*John*, i. 14.

God sent the Archangel Gabriel to ask Mary's consent that he should become her Son; Mary gives her consent, and behold the Word is made man. O wonderful prodigy! at which the heavens and all nature stand in astonishment! The Word made flesh! A God made man! What if we were to see a king become a worm, to save the life of a little worm of earth by his death?

So, then, my Jesus, Thou art my God, and not being able to die as God, Thou hast been pleased to become man capable of dying in order to give Thy life for me. My sweet Redeemer, how is it that, at the sight of such mercy and love Thou hast shown towards me, I do not die of grief? Thou didst come down from heaven to seek me, a lost sheep; and how many times have I not driven Thee away, preferring my miserable pleasures before Thee! But since Thou dost wish to have me, I leave all; I wish to be Thine, and I will have none other but Thee. Thee do I choose for the only object of my affections. *My Beloved to me, and I to Him.*[1] Thou dost think of me, and I will think of none but Thee. Let me always love Thee, and may I never leave off loving Thee. Provided I can love Thee, I am content to be deprived of all sensible consolation, and even to suffer all torments. I see that Thou dost indeed wish me to be all Thine, and I wish to belong entirely to Thee. I know that everything in the world is a falsehood, a deceit, nothing but smoke, filth, and vanity. Thou alone art the true and only good; therefore Thou alone art sufficient for me. *My God, I wish for Thee alone, and nothing else*; God hear me, *for Thee alone do I wish, and nothing else.*

## VIII.

*Semetipsum exinanivit.*

"He emptied Himself."—*Phil.* ii. 7.

Behold the only-begotton Son of God, omnipotent and true God, equal to the Father, born a little Infant in a stable. *He emptied Himself, taking the form of a servant, being made to the likeness of men.*[2] If any one would see a God annihilated, let him enter into the cave of Bethlehem, and he will find him as a little Infant, bound in swaddling-clothes, so that he cannot move, weeping and trembling with cold. Ah, holy faith, tell me whose Son is this poor child? Faith answers, he is the Son of God, and he is true God. And who has brought him to so miserable a condition? It was the love he had for men. And yet there are men to be found who do not love this God!

---

[1] *Cant.* ii. 16.

[2] *Phil.* ii. 7.

Thou, then, my Jesus, hast spent all Thy life amidst sorrows to make me understand the love Thou dost bear me, and I have spent my life in despising and displeasing Thee by my sins! Ah, make me know the evil I have committed, and the love which Thou desirest to have. But since Thou hast borne with me till now, permit me not to give Thee any more cause for sorrow. Inflame me altogether with Thy love, and remind me always of all Thou hast suffered for me, that from this day forth I may forget everything, and think of nothing but loving and pleasing Thee. Thou didst come on earth to reign in our hearts; take, then, from my heart all that could prevent Thee from possessing it entirely! Make my will to be wholy conformed to Thy will; may Thine be mine, and may it be the rule of all my actions and desires.

## IX.

*Parvulus natus est nobis, et Filius datus est nobis.*

"For a child is born to us, and a Son is given to us."—*Isa.* ix. 6.

Behold the end for which the Son of God will be born an Infant, to give himself to us from his childhood, and thus to draw to himself our love. Why (writes St. Francis de Sales) does Jesus take the sweet and tender form of an Infant, if it be not to stimulate us to love him and to confide in him? St. Peter Chrysologus had said before, "Thus he willed to be born, because he wished to be loved."

Oh, dear child Jesus, my Saviour! I love Thee, in Thee do I trust, Thou art all my hope and all my love. What would have become of me if Thou hadst not come down from heaven to save me? I know the hell which would have awaited me for the offences I have offered Thee. Blessed be Thy mercy, because Thou art ever ready to pardon me if I repent of my sins. Yes, I repent with all my heart, my Jesus, of having despised Thee. Receive me into Thy favor, and make me die to myself to live only to Thee, my only good. Destroy in me, O thou consuming fire, everything that is displeasing in Thine eyes, and draw all my affections to Thee. I love Thee, O God of my soul, I love Thee, my treasure, my life, my all. I love Thee, and I wish to die saying, my God, I love Thee; and begin then to love Thee with a perfect love which shall have no end.

## X.

*Rorate, cœli, desuper, et nubes pluant Justum.—Emitte Agnum, Domine, dominatorem terrœ.—Salutare tuum da nobis.*

"Drop down dew, O ye heavens, from above, and let the clouds rain the just."—"Send forth the Lamb, the Ruler of the earth."—*Isa.* xlv. 8; xvi. 1. —"Grant us Thy salvation."—*Ps.* lxxxiv. 8.

Thus did the holy Prophets desire for so many years the coming of the Saviour. The same prophet Isaias said: *Oh, that Thou wouldst send the heavens, and wouldst come down: the mountains would melt away at Thy presence, . . . the waters would burn with fire.*[1] Lord, he said, when men shall see that Thou hast come on earth out of love for them, the mountains shall be made smooth, that is, men in serving Thee will conquer all the difficulties that at first appeared to them insuperable obstacles. The waters

[1] *Isa.* lxiv. 1, 2.

would burn with fire, and the coldest hearts will feel themselves burning with Thy love, at the sight of Thee made man, and how well has this been verified in many happy souls!—in St. Teresa, in St. Philip Neri, St. Francis Xavier, who even in this life were consumed by this holy fire. But how many such are there? Alas! but too few.

Ah, my Jesus, amongst these few I wish also to be. How many years ought I not already be burning in hell, separated from Thee, hating and cursing Thee forever. But no, Thou hast borne with me with so much patience, that Thou mightest see me burn, not with that unhappy flame, but with the blessed fire of Thy love; for this end Thou hast given me so many illuminations, and hast so often wounded my heart while I was far from Thee; finally, Thou hast done so much that Thou hast forced me to love Thee by Thy sweet attractions. Behold, I am now Thine. I will be Thine always and altogether. It remains for Thee to make me faithful, and this I confidently hope from Thy goodness. O my God! who could ever have the heart to leave Thee again and to live even a moment without Thy love? I love Thee, my Jesus, above all things; but this is little. I love Thee more than myself, but this is little also; I love Thee with all my heart, and this also is little. My Jesus, hear me, give me more love, more love, more love. O Mary, pray to God for me.

## XI.

*Despectum, et novissimum virorum.*

"Despised, and the most abject of men."—*Isa.* liii. 3.

Behold what was the life of the Son of God made man, the most abject of men. He was treated as the vilest, the least of men. To what extreme of meanness could the life of Christ be reduced greater than that of being born in a stable? of living as a servant in an unknown and despised shop? struck, treated as a mock king, having his face spit upon? and, finally, of dying condemned as a malefactor on an infamous gibbet?

St. Bernard exclaims, "Oh, lowest and highest!" A God, Thou art the Lord of all, and how art Thou contented to be the most despised of all? And I, my Jesus, when I see Thee so humiliated for me, how can I wish to be esteemed and honored by all? A sinner to be proud! Ah, my despised Redeemer, may Thy example inspire me with love of contempt and of an obscure life; from this time forward I hope, with Thy help, to accept from my heart all opprobrium that I may have to suffer for the love of Thee, who hast endured so much for the love of me. Pardon me the pride of my past life, and give me love in its place. I love Thee, my despised Jesus. Go before me with Thy cross. I will follow Thee with mine, and I will not leave Thee till I die crucified for Thee, as Thou didst die crucified for me. My Jesus, my despised Jesus, I embrace Thee; in Thy embrace will I live and die.

## XII.

Virum dolorum.

"A man of sorrows."—*Isa.* liii. 3.

What was the life of Jesus Christ? A life of sorrows; a life of internal and external sorrows from the beginning to the end. But what most afflicted Jesus Christ during the course of his life was the sight of the sins and the ingratitude with which men repaid the pains he had suffered with so much love for us. This thought had made him the most afflicted amongst all men that had ever lived on the earth.

So, then, my Jesus, I also added to the affliction Thou didst suffer during the whole of Thy life by my sins. And why do I not also say, as did St. Margaret of Cortona, who, when exhorted by her confessor to calm her grief and not to weep any more because God had pardoned her, redoubled her tears and answered, "Ah, my Father, how can I leave off weeping when I know that my sins afflicted my Jesus through the whole of his life?" Oh that I could die of grief, my Jesus, whenever I think of all the bitter anguish I have caused Thee every day of my life! Alas, how many nights have I slept deprived of Thy grace! How many times hast Thou pardoned me, and I have again turned my back upon Thee! My dear Lord, I repent above all things for having offended Thee. I love Thee with all my heart; I love Thee with all my soul. "Ah, my sweet Jesus, permit me not to be separated any more from Thee." Let me die rather than betray Thee afresh. Mary, Mother of perseverance, obtain for me the gift of holy perseverance.

## XIII.

*Cum dilexisset suos, qui erant in mundo, in finem dilexit eos.*

"Having loved his own who were in the world, He loved them unto the end."—*John*, xiii. i.

The love of friends increases at the time of death, when they are on the point of being separated from those they love; and it is then, therefore, that they try more than ever, by some pledge of affection, to show the love they bear to them. Jesus during the whole of his life gave us marks of his affection, but when he came near the hour of his death he wished to give us a special proof of his love. For what greater proof could this loving Lord show us than by giving his blood and his life for each of us? And not content with this, he left this very same body, sacrificed for us upon the cross, to be our food, so that each one who should receive it should be wholly united to him, and thus love should mutually increase.

O infinite goodness! O infinite love! Ah, my enamoured Jesus, fill my heart with Thy love, so that I may forget the world and myself, to think of nothing but loving and pleasing Thee. I consecrate to Thee my body, my soul, my will, my liberty. Up to this time I have sought to gratify myself to Thy great displeasure; I am exceedingly sorry for it, my crucified love; hence forth I will seek nothing but Thee, my God and my all. My God, Thou art my all, I wish for Thee alone and nothing more. Oh that I could spend myself all for Thee, who hast spent Thyself all for me! I love Thee, my only good, my only love. I love Thee, and abandon myself entirely to Thy holy will. Make me love Thee, and then do with me what Thou wilt.

## XIV.

*Tristis est anima mea usque ad mortem.*

"My soul is sorrowful even unto death."—*Matt.* xxvi. 38.

These were the words that proceeded from the sorrowful heart of Jesus Christ in the garden of Gethsemani, before he went to die. Alas, whence came this extreme grief of his, which was so great that it was enough to kill him? Perhaps it was on account of the torments that he saw he should have to surfer? No; for he had foreseen these torments from the time of his incarnation. He had foreseen them, and had accepted them of his own free will: *He was offered because it was His own will.*[1] His grief came from seeing the sins men would commit after his death. It was then, according to St. Bernardine of Sienna, that he saw clearly each particular sin of each one of us. He had regard to every individual sin.

It was not, then, my Jesus, the sight of the scourges, of the thorns, and of the cross which so afflicted Thee in the garden of Gethsemani; it was the sight of my sins, each one of which so oppressed Thy heart with grief and sadness that it made Thee agonize and sweat blood. This is the recompense I have made Thee for the love Thou hast shown me by dying for me. Ah, let me share the grief Thou didst feel in the garden for my sins, so that the remembrance of

[1] *Isa.* liii. 7.

it may make me sad for all my life. Ah, my sweet Redeemer, if I could but console Thee as much now by my grief and love as I then afflicted Thee! I repent, my Love, with all my heart for having preferred my own miserable satisfaction to Thee. I am sorry, and I love Thee above all things. Although I have despised Thee, yet I hear Thee ask for my love. Thou wouldst have me love Thee with all my heart: *Love the Lord thy God with all thy heart, and with all thy soul.*[1] Yes, my God, I love Thee with all my heart, I love Thee with all my soul. Do Thou give me the love Thou requirest of me. If I have hitherto sought myself, I will now seek none but Thee. And seeing that Thou hast loved me more than others, more than others will I love Thee. Draw me always more, my Jesus, to Thy love by the odor of Thy ointments, which are the loving attractions of Thy grace. Finally, give me strength to correspond to so much love which God has borne to an ungrateful worm and traitor. Mary, Mother of mercy, help me by thy prayers.

## XV.

*Comprehenderunt Jesum, et ligaverunt eum.*

"They took Jesus and bound him."—*John*, xviii. 12.

A God taken and bound! What could the angels have said at seeing their king with his hands bound, led between soldiers through the streets of Jerusalem! And what ought we to say at the sight of our God, who is content for our sake to be bound as a thief, to be presented to the judge who is to condemn

---

[1] *Matt.* xxii. 37.

him to death? St. Bernard laments, saying, "What hast Thou to do with chains?" What have malefactors and chains to do with Thee, O my Jesus, Thou who art infinite goodness and majesty? They should belong to us sinners, guilty of hell, and not to Thee who art innocent and the Holy of holies. St. Bernard goes on to say, on seeing Jesus guilty of death, "What hast Thou done, my innocent Saviour, that Thou shouldst be thus condemned?" O my dear Saviour, Thou art innocence itself; for what crime hast Thou been thus condemned? Ah, I will tell Thee, he replies: the crime Thou hast committed is the too great lover Thou hast borne to men. Thy sin is love.

My beloved Jesus, I kiss the cords that bind Thee, for they have freed me from those eternal chains which I have deserved. Alas! how many times have I renounced Thy friendship and made myself a slave of Satan, dishonoring Thy infinite majesty! I grieve above all things for having so grievously insulted Thee. Ah, my God, bind my will to Thy feet with the sweet cords of Thy holy love, that it may wish for nothing but what is pleasing to Thee. May I take Thy will for the sole guide of my life. As Thou hast had so great care for my good, may I not care for anything but to love Thee. I love Thee, my sovereign Good; I love Thee, the only object of my affections. I know that Thou alone hast loved me truly, and Thee alone will I love. I renounce everything. Thou alone art sufficient for me.

## XVI.

*Ipse autem vulneratus est propter iniquitates nostras, attritus est propter scelera nostra.*

"But He was wounded for our iniquities, He was bruised for our sins."—*Isa.* liii. 5.

One single blow suffered by this Man-God was sufficient for the sins of the whole world; but Jesus Christ was not satisfied with that; he wished to be *wounded and bruised* for our iniquities, which means to say, wounded and torn from head to foot, so that there should be no whole part remaining in his sacred body. Hence the same prophet beheld him full of sores like a leper. *And we have thought Him as it were a leper, and as one struck by God and afflicted.*[1]

O wounds of my sorrowful Jesus, you are all living evidences of the love which my Redeemer preserves for me; with tender words do you force me to love him for the many sufferings that he has undergone for the love of me. All, my sweet Jesus, when shall I give myself all to Thee, as Thou hast given Thyself all to me? I love Thee, my sovereign good. I love Thee, my God, lover of my soul. O God of love, give me love. By my love let me atone to Thee for the bitterness I have given Thee in times past. Help me to drive from my heart everything that does not tend to Thy love. Eternal Father, *look at the face of Thy Christ,*[2] look at the wounds of Thy Son, which seek pity for me, and for their sake pardon me the outrages that I have

[1] *Isa.* liii. 4.

[2] *Ps.* lxxxiii. 10.

committed against Thee; take my heart entirely to Thyself, that it may not love, seek, nor sigh after any other but Thee. I say to Thee, with St. Ignatius, "Give me only love of Thee and Thy grace and I am rich enough." Behold this is all I ask of Thee, O God of my soul; give me Thy love, together with Thy grace, and I desire nothing else. O Mary, Mother of God, intercede for me.

## XVII.

*Ave, Rex Judæorum.*

"Hail, King of the Jews."—*Matt.* xxvii. 29.

Thus was our Redeemer scornfully saluted by the Roman soldiers. After having treated him as a false king, and having crowned him with thorns, they knelt before him and called him king of the Jews, and then, rising up with loud cries and laughter, they struck him and spit in his face. St. Matthew writes: *And platting a crown of thorns, they put it on His head. . . . And bowing the knee before Him, they mocked Him, saying, Hail, King of the Jews; and spitting upon Him they took the reed and struck His head.*[1] And St. John adds, *And they gave Him blows.*[2]

O my Jesus! this barbarous crown that encircles Thy head, this vile reed that Thou dost hold in Thy hand, this torn purple garment that covers Thee with ridicule, make Thee known indeed as a king, but a king of love. The Jews will not acknowledge Thee for their king, and they say to Pilate, *We have no King*

[1] *Matt.* xxvii. 29.

[2] *John*, xix. 3.

*but Cæsar.*[1] My beloved Redeemer, if others will not have Thee for their king, I accept Thee, and desire that Thou shouldst be the only King of my soul. To Thee do I consecrate my whole self; dispose of me as Thou pleasest. For this end hast Thou endured contempt, so many sorrows, and death itself, to gain our hearts and to reign therein by Thy love. *For this end Christ died, . . . that he might be Lord both of the dead and of the living.*[2] Make Thyself, therefore, master of my heart, O my beloved King, and reign and exercise Thy sway there forever. Formerly I refused Thee for my Lord, that I might serve my passions; now I will be all Thine and Thee alone will I serve. Ah, bind me to Thee by Thy love, and make me always remember the bitter death that Thou hast willed to suffer for me. Ah, my King, my God, my love, my all, what do I wish for if not for Thee alone!—*Thee, God of my heart, and my portion forever.*[3] O God of my heart! I love Thee; Thou art my portion, Thou art my only good.

## XVIII.

*Et bajulans sibi crucem, exivit in eum, qui dicitur Calvariæ, locum.*

"And bearing His own Cross, He went forth to that place which is called Calvary."—*John*, xix. 17.

Behold the Saviour of the world has now set out on his journey with his cross on his shoulders, going forth to die in torments for the love of men. The divine Lamb allows himself to be led without

[1] *John*, xix. 15.

[2] *Rom.* xiv. 9.

[3] *Ps.* lxxii. 26.

complaining, to be sacrificed upon the cross for our salvation. Go thou, also, my soul, accompany and follow thy Jesus, who goes to suffer death for thy love, to satisfy for thy sins. Tell me, my Jesus and my God, what dost Thou expect from men by giving Thy life for their sake? St. Bernard answers, Thou dost expect nothing but to be loved by them: "When God loves, he wishes for nothing but to be loved in return."

Is it, then, my Redeemer, at so great a cost that Thou hast desired to gain our love? And shall there be any among men who believe in Thee, and not love Thee? I comfort myself with the thought that Thou art the love of all the souls of the saints, the love of Mary, the love of Thy Father; but, O my God, how many are there who will not know Thee, and how many that know Thee and yet will not love Thee! Infinite Love, make Thy self known, make Thyself loved. Ah, that I could by my blood and my death make Thee loved by all! But alas that I have lived so many years in the world while I knew Thee, but did not love Thee! But now at last Thou hast drawn me to love Thee by Thy so great goodness. At one time I was so unhappy as to lose Thy grace; but the grief I now feel for it, the desire of being all Thine, and still more the death Thou hast suffered for me, give me a firm confidence, O my Love, that Thou hast already pardoned me, and that now Thou dost love me. Oh that I could die for Thee, my Jesus, as Thou hast died for me! Although no punishment awaited those who love Thee not, I would never leave off loving Thee, and I would do all I could to please Thee. Thou who givest me this good desire, give me strength to follow it out. My love, my hope, do not abandon me; make me correspond, during the remainder of my life to the especial love that Thou has borne me. Thou desirest to have me for Thine own, and I wish to be all for Thee. I love Thee, my God, my treasure, my all. I will live and die always repeating, I love Thee, I love Thee, I love Thee.

XIX.

*Quasi agnus coram tondente se, obmutescet, et non aperiet os suum.*

"And shall be dumb as a lamb before his shearer, and He shall not open his mouth."—*Is.* liii. 7.

This was precisely the passage which the eunuch of Queen Candace was reading; but not understanding of whom it was written, St. Philip, inspired by God, entered the carriage in which the eunuch was, and explained to him that these words referred to our Redeemer Jesus Christ. Jesus was called a lamb because he was dragged into the prætorium of Pilate, and then led to death just like an innocent lamb. Therefore the Baptist calls him a lamb. *Behold the Lamb of God, behold Him who taketh away the sins of the world.*[1] A lamb who suffers and dies a victim on the cross for our sins. *Surely he hath borne our infirmities and carried our sorrows.*[2] Miserable are those who do not love Jesus Christ during their life. In the last day the sight of this Lamb in his wrath will make them say to the mountains, *Fall upon us*

---

[1] *John*, i. 29.

[2] *Isa.* liii. 4.

*and hide us from the face of Him that sitteth upon the throne, and from the wrath of the Lamb.*[1]

No, my divine Lamb, if in times past I have not loved Thee, now I will love Thee forever. Before, I was blind; but now that thou hast enlightened me, and hast made me know the great evil I have done in turning my back upon Thee, and the infinite love which is due to Thee for Thy goodness and for the love Thou hast borne me, I repent with all my heart for having offended Thee, and I love Thee above all things. O wounds, O blood of my Redeemer, how many souls have you not inflamed with love! inflame my soul also. Ah, my Jesus, continually call to my remembrance Thy Passion and the pains and ignominies that Thou hast suffered for me, that I may detach my affections from earthly goods and place them all on Thee, my only and infinite good. I love Thee, Lamb of God, sacrificed and annihilated on the cross for my sake. Thou hast not refused to suffer for me; I will not refuse to suffer for Thee whatever Thou requirest. I will no longer complain of the crosses that Thou dost send me. I ought to have been in hell these many years; how, then, can I complain? Give me grace to love Thee, and then do with me what Thou wilt. *Who shall separate me from the love of Christ?*[2] Ah, my Jesus, sin alone can separate me from Thy love. Ah, let it not be; rather let me die a thousand times; this I beg of Thee by Thy sacred

[1] *Apoc.* vi. 16.
[2] *Rom.* viii. 35.

Passion. I beseech thee, Mary, by thy sorrows deliver me from the death of sin.

XX.

*Deus meus! Deus meus! ut quid dereliquisti me?*
"My God, my God, why hast Thou forsaken me?"—*Matt.* xxvii. 46.

O God! who shall not compassionate the Son of God, who for love of men is dying of grief on a cross? He is tormented externally in his body by the innumerable wounds, and internally he is so afflicted and sad that he seeks solace for his great sorrow from the Eternal Father; but his Father, in order to satisfy his divine justice, abandons him, and leaves him to die desolate and deprived of every consolation.

O desolate death of my dear Redeemer, Thou art my hope. O my abandoned Jesus, Thy merits make me hope that I shall not remain abandoned and separated from Thee forever in hell. I do not care to live in consolation on this earth; I embrace all the pains and desolations that Thou mayest send me. He is not worthy of consolation who by offending Thee has merited for himself eternal torments. It is enough for me to love Thee and to live in Thy grace. This alone do I beg of Thee, let me nevermore see myself deprived of Thy love. Let me be abandoned by all; do not Thou abandon me in this extremity. I love Thee, my Jesus, who didst die abandoned for me. I love Thee, my only good, my only hope, my only love.

## XXI.

*Crucifixerunt eum, et cum eo alios duos hinc et hinc, medium autem Jesum.*
"They crucified Him, and with Him two others, one on each side, and Jesus in the midst."—*John*, xix. 18.

The incarnate Word was called by the sacred spouse, *All lovely; such is my beloved.*[1] At whatever period of his life Jesus Christ presents himself to us, he appears altogether desirable and most worthy of love, whether we see him as an infant in the stable, as a boy in the shop of St. Joseph, as a solitary meditating in the desert, or bathed in sweat as he walked about preaching throughout Judea. But in no other form does he appear more loving than when he is nailed to the cross on which the immense love he bears us forced him to die. St. Francis de Sales has said, the Mount of Calvary is the hill of lovers. All love which does not take its rise from the Passion of the Saviour is weak. How miserable is the death where there is no love of the Redeemer! Let us stop, then, and consider that this man, nailed to the tree of shame, is our true God, and that he is here suffering and dying for nothing but for the love of us.

Ah, my Jesus, if all men would stand still and contemplate Thee on the cross, believing with a lively faith, that Thou art their God, and that Thou hast died for their salvation, how could they live far from Thee and without Thy love? And how could I, knowing all this, have displeased Thee so often? If others have offended Thee, they have at least sinned in

---

[1] *Cant.* v. 16.

darkness; but I have sinned in the light. But these pierced hands, this wounded side, this blood, these wounds which I see in Thee, make me hope for pardon and Thy grace. I am grieved, my Love, for having ever so despised Thee. But now I love Thee with all my heart; and my greatest grief is the remembrance of my having despised Thee. This grief, however, which I feel, is a sign that Thou hast pardoned me. O burning heart of my Jesus, inflame my poor heart with Thy love. O my Jesus, dead, consumed with sorrow for me, make me die consumed with sorrow for having offended Thee, and with the love Thou dost merit, I sacrifice myself entirely to Thee, who hast sacrificed Thyself entirely for me. O sorrowful Mother Mary, make me faithful in loving Jesus!

## XXII.

*Et inclinato capite, tradidit spiritum.*

"And bowing His head, He gave up the ghost."—*John*, xix. 30.

Behold, my Redeemer, to what Thy love for men has brought Thee even to die of sorrow on a cross, drowned in a sea of grief and ignominy; as David had predicted of Thee. *I am come into the depth of the sea, and a tempest hath overwhelmed me.*[1] St. Francis de Sales writes thus: "Let us contemplate this divine Saviour stretched on the cross, as upon the altar of his glory, on which he is dying of love for us. Ah, why, then, do we not in spirit throw ourselves upon him to die upon the cross with him who has chosen to die there for the love of us? I will hold him, we

[1] *Ps.* lxvii. 3.

ought to say; I will never let him go. I will die with him, and will burn in the flames of his love; one and the same fire shall devour this divine Creator and his miserable creature. My Jesus is all mine, and I am all his. I will live and die on his bosom. Neither life nor death shall ever separate me from my Jesus."

Yes, my dear Redeemer, I hold fast to Thy cross; I kiss Thy pierced feet, touched with compassion and confounded at seeing the affection with which Thou hast died for me. Ah, accept me, and bind me to Thy feet, that I may no more depart from Thee, and may from this day forward converse with Thee alone, consult with Thee on all my thoughts; in a word, may I henceforth direct all my affections so as to seek nothing but to love Thee and please Thee, always longing to leave this valley of dangers to come and love Thee face to face with all my strength in Thy kingdom, which is a kingdom of eternal love. In the meantime let me always live, grieving for the offences I have committed against Thee, and always burning with love for Thee, who for love of me hast given Thy life. I love Thee, my Jesus, who hast died for me; I love Thee, O infinite lover; I love Thee, O infinite love; I love Thee, infinite goodness. O Mary, Mother of beautiful love, pray to my Jesus for me.

## XXIII.

*Oblatus est, quia ipse voluit.*

"He was offered because it was His own will."—*Isa.* liii. 7 .

The incarnate Word, at the moment of his conception, saw before him all the souls that he was to redeem. Then thou also, my soul, wast presented with the guilt of all thy sins upon thee, and for thee did Jesus Christ accept all the pains that he suffered in life and death; and in doing so he obtained for thee thy pardon, and all the graces that thou hast received from God the lights, the calls of his love, the helps to overcome temptations, the spiritual consolations, the tears, the compassionate feelings thou hast experienced when thinking of the love he had for thee, and the sentiments of sorrow in remembering how thou hast offended him.

Thou didst, then, my Jesus, from the very beginning of Thy life, take upon Thee all my sins, and didst offer Thyself to satisfy for them by Thy sufferings. By Thy death Thou hast delivered me from eternal death: *But Thou hast delivered my soul, that it should not perish; Thou hast cast all my sins behind Thy back.*[1] Thou, my love, instead of punishing me for the insults which I have added to those that Thou hadst already received, hast gone on adding to Thy favors and mercies towards me, in order to win my heart one day to Thyself. My Jesus, this day is come; I love Thee with all my soul. Who should love Thee if I do not? This is the first sin, my Jesus, that Thou hast to forgive me, that I have been so many years in the world without loving Thee. But for the future I will do all I can to please Thee. I feel by Thy grace a great desire to live to Thee alone, and to detach myself from all created things, I have also a great compunction for the displeasure that I have caused Thee. This desire and this sorrow, I see, my Jesus,

[1] *Isa.* xxxviii. 17.

are all Thy gift. Continue, then, my love, to keep me faithful in Thy love; for Thou knowest my weakness. Make me all Thine, as Thou hast made Thyself all mine. I love Thee, my only good; I love Thee, my only love; I love Thee, my treasure, my all; My Jesus, I love Thee, I love Thee, I love Thee. Help me, O Mother of God.

## XXIV.

*Deus Filium suum mittens in similitudinem carnis peccati, et de peccato damnavit peccatum in carne. Christus nos redemit de maledicto legis factus pro nobis maledictum, quia scriptum est: Maledictus omnis qui pendet in ligno.*

"God sending his own Son in the likeness of sinful flesh, even of sin, hath condemned sin in the flesh."—*Rom.* viii. 3. "Christ hath redeemed us from the curse of the law, being made a curse for us, for it is written: Cursed is every one that hangeth on a tree."—*Gal.* iii. 73.

Hence we see that Jesus Christ willed to appear in the world as a guilty and an accused man, hanging on the cross to deliver us from eternal malediction.

O eternal Father, for the love of this Son so dear to Thee, have pity on me! And Thou, Jesus, my Redeemer, who by Thy death hast liberated me from the slavery of sin in which I was born, and of the sins that I have committed since my baptism, ah, change the miserable chains which once bound me a slave to Satan into chains of gold, which may bind me to Thee with a holy love. Arise and show forth in me the efficacy of Thy merits, by changing me, a sinner, into a saint. I have deserved to be burning in hell for many years past: but I hope by Thy infinite mercy, for the glory of Thy death, to burn with Thy love, and to be all Thine. I wish that my heart should love none but Thee. *Thy kingdom come.* Reign, my Jesus, reign over my whole soul. May it obey Thee alone, seek Thee alone, desire Thee alone. Away from my heart, ye earthly affections! and come, O ye flames of divine love; come and remain alone to possess and consume me for that God of love who didst die consumed for me. I love Thee, my Jesus; I love Thee, O infinite Sweetness and my true lover, I have no one who has loved me more than Thou; and therefore I give and consecrate myself to Thee, my treasure and my all.

## XXV.

*Dilexit nos, et lavit nos a peccatis nostris in sanguine suo.*

"He hath loved us. and washed us from our sins in His own blood."—*Apoc.* i. 5.

So, then, my Jesus, in order to save my soul, Thou hast prepared a bath of Thine own blood wherein to cleanse it from the filth of its sins. If, then, our souls have been bought by Thy blood, *For you are bought with a great price,*[1] it is a sign that Thou lovest them much; and as Thou dost love them, let us pray thus to Thee: *We therefore pray Thee to help Thy servants, whom Thou hast redeemed with Thy precious blood.* It is true that by my sins I have separated myself from Thee, and have knowingly lost Thee. But remember, my Jesus, that Thou hast bought me with Thy blood. Ah, may this blood not have been given in vain for me, which was shed with so much grief and so much love.

By my sins I have driven Thee, my God, from my soul, and have merited Thy hatred; but Thou hast said that Thou wouldst forget the crimes of a

[1] 1 *Cor.* vi. 20.

repentant sinner. *But if he do penance . . . I will not remember all his iniquities.*[1] Thou hast further said, *I love them that love me.*[2] I pray Thee, therefore, my Jesus, to forget all the injuries that I have offered Thee, and love me; whilst I also will now love Thee more than myself, and repent above all things for having offended Thee. Ah, my beloved Lord, for the sake of that blood which Thou hast shed for the love of me, hate me no longer, but love me. It is not enough for me that Thou shouldst only forgive me the chastisement I deserve, I desire to love Thee and to be loved by Thee. O God, who art all love, all goodness, unite me and bind me to Thyself, and permit not that I should ever be separated from Thee any more, and that thus I should deserve Thy hatred. No, my Jesus, my love, let it not be, I will be all Thine, and I desire that Thou shouldst be all mine.

## XXVI.

*Humiliavit semetipsum, factus obediens usque ad mortem, mortem autem crucis.*

"He humbled Himself, becoming obedient unto death; even the death of the cross."—*Phil.* ii. 8.

What great thing is that the martyrs have done in giving their lives for God, while this God has humbled himself to the death of the cross for their love? To render a just return for the death of a God, it would not be sufficient to sacrifice the lives of all men; the death of another God for his love would alone compensate for it. O my Jesus! allow me, a poor

[1] *Ezek.* xviii. 21.

[2] *Prov.* viii. 17.

sinner, to say to Thee, with Thy true lover St. Francis of Assisi, "May I die, O Lord, for the love of Thy love, as Thou didst deign to die for the love of my love."

Is it true, my Redeemer, that hitherto, for the love of my own pleasures, unhappy that I am! I have renounced Thy love? Would that I had died before, and had never offended Thee! I thank Thee that Thou givest me time to love Thee in this life, that I may afterwards love Thee throughout all eternity. Ah, remind me continually, my Jesus, of the ignominious death that Thou hast suffered for me, that I may never forget to love Thee in consideration of the love that Thou hast borne me. I love Thee, infinite goodness; I love Thee, my supreme good; to Thee I give myself entirely, and by that love which caused Thee to die for me, do Thou accept my love, and let me die, destroy me, rather than ever permit me to leave off loving Thee. I will say to Thee, with St. Francis de Sales, "O eternal Love, my soul seeks Thee, and chooses Thee for all eternity. Come, O Holy Spirit, inflame our hearts with Thy love. Either to love or to die. To die to all other affections, to live only to the love of Jesus."

## XXVII.

*Charitas enim Chiristi urget nos.*

"The Charity of Christ presseth us."—2. *Cor.* v. 14.

How tender and full of unction are the words with which St. Francis de Sales comments on this passage in his book of the divine love! "Hear Theotimus," he says; "nothing forces and presses the soul of man so much as love. If a man knows that he is loved by any one, he feels himself forced to love him; but if a peasant is loved by a lord, he is still more strongly forced; and if by a monarch, how much more so! Know, then, that Jesus, the true God, has loved us so far as to suffer death, even the death of the cross for us. Is not this to have our hearts put under a press, and to feel them squeezed and crushed so as to force out our love with a violence which is all the stronger for being so loving."

Ah, my Jesus, since Thou dost desire to be loved by me, remind me always of the love that Thou hast borne me, and of the pains Thou hast suffered to show me this love. May the remembrance of them be ever present in my mind and in the minds of all men, for it is impossible to believe what Thou hast suffered to oblige us to love, and yet not love Thee. Till now the cause of my negligent and wicked life has been, that I have not thought of the affection which Thou, my Jesus, hast had for me. All this time, however, I knew the great displeasure my sins gave Thee, and nevertheless I went on multiplying them. Every time I remember this I should wish to die of grief for it, and I should not now have courage to ask Thy pardon, if I did not know that Thou didst die to obtain forgiveness for me. Thou hast borne with me in order that at the sight of the wrong I have done Thee, and of the death that Thou hast suffered for me, my sorrow and love towards Thee should be increased. I repent, my dear Redeemer, with all my heart, for having offended Thee, and I love Thee with all my soul. After so many signs of Thy affection, and after the many mercies that Thou hast shown me, I promise Thee that I will love none but Thee. Thee will I love with all my strength; Thou art my Jesus, my love, my all. Thou art my love, because in Thee I have placed all my affections Thou art my all, because I will have none other but Thee. Grant, then, that always, both in life and death and through all eternity, I may ever call Thee my God, my love, and my all.

## XXVIII.

*Charitas enim Christi urget nos.*

"The charity of Christ presseth us."—2 *Cor*. v. 14.

Let us consider anew the force of these words. The Apostle means to say that it is not so much the thought of all that Christ has suffered for us that should constrain us to love him, as the thought of the love that he has shown us in wishing to suffer so much for us. This love made our Saviour say, while he was yet alive, that he was dying with the desire that the day of his death should draw near to make us know the boundless love that he had for us. *I have a baptism wherewith I am to be baptized, and how am I straitened till it be accomplished!* [1] And the same love made him say the last night of his life. *With desire, I have desired to eat this pasch with you before I suffer.*[2]

So great, then, my Jesus, was the desire that Thou hadst to be loved by us, that all through Thy life Thou didst desire nothing but to suffer and to die for us, and so to put us under the necessity of loving Thee at

[1] *Luke*, xii. 50.

[2] *Ibid*. xxii. 15.

least out of gratitude for so much love. Dost Thou so thirst for our love? How is it, then, that we so little desire Thine. Alas, that I should have been up to this time so foolish! Not only have I not desired Thy love, but I have brought down upon myself Thy hatred by losing my respect for Thee. My dear Redeemer, I know the evil I have done, I detest it above all my other sins, and am sorry from the bottom of my heart. Now I desire Thy love more than all the goods of the world. My best and only treasure, I love Thee above all things, I love Thee more than myself, I love Thee with all my soul, and I desire nothing but to love Thee and to be loved by Thee. Forget, my Jesus, the offences that I have committed against Thee; do Thou also love me, and love me exceedingly, that I may exceedingly love Thee. Thou art my love, Thou art my hope, Thou knowest how weak I am; help me, Jesus, my love; help me, Jesus, my hope. Succor me also with thy prayers, O Mary, great Mother of God.

## XXIX.

*Majorem hac dilcctionem nemo habet, ut animam suam ponat quis pro amicis suis.*

"Greater love than this no man hath, that a man lay down his life for his friends."—*John*, xv. 13.

What more, O my soul! could thy God do than to give his life in order to make thee love him? To give his life is the greatest mark of affection that a man can give to another man who is his friend. But what love must that have been which our Creator has shown to us, in choosing to die for us his creatures! This is what St. John was considering when he wrote: *In this we have known the charity of God, because He hath laid down His life for us.*[1] Indeed, if faith did not teach us that a God has willed to die to show us his love, who would ever have been able to believe it?

Ah, my Jesus, I believe that Thou hast died for me, and therefore I confess that I deserve a thousand hells for having repaid with insults and ingratitude the love that Thou hast borne me in giving Thy life for me. I thank Thy mercy, which has promised to forgive those that repent. Trusting, then, in this sweet promise, I hope for pardon from Thee, repenting, as I do, with all my heart for having so often despised Thy love. But since Thy love has not abandoned me, overcome by Thy love I consecrate myself all to Thee. Thou, my Jesus, hast finished Thy life by dying in agony on a cross; and what recompense can I, a miserable creature, make Thee? I consecrate to Thee my life, accepting with love all the sufferings that will come to me from Thy hand, both in life and in death. Softened and confounded at the great mercy that Thou hast used towards me, I hold fast Thy cross; at Thy feet will I thus live and die. Ah, my Redeemer, by the love that Thou hast borne me in dying for me, do not permit me ever to separate myself from Thee again. Make me always live and die in Thy embrace. My Jesus, my Jesus, I repeat, make me always live and die united with Thee.

---

[1] 1 *John*, iii. 16.

## XXX.

*Et ego, si exaltatus fuero a terra, omnia traham ad me ipsum.*

"I, if I be lifted up from the earth, will draw all things unto Myself."—*John*, xii.. 32.

Thou hast said, then, my Saviour, that when hanging on the cross Thou wouldst draw all our hearts unto Thyself; why is it that for so many years my heart has gone far away from Thee? Ah, it is not Thy fault. How many times hast Thou called me to Thy love and I have turned a deaf ear? How many times too hast Thou pardoned me, and affectionately warned me by remorse of conscience not to offend Thee again, and I have repeated my offence? Ah, my Jesus, send me not to hell, because there I shall be cursing forever these graces which Thou hast given me; so that these graces, the illuminations Thou hast given me, Thy calls, Thy patience in bearing with me, the blood that Thou didst shed to save me, would be the most cruel of all the torments of hell. But now I bear Thee call me again, and Thou dost say to me, with the greatest love, as if I had never offended Thee: *Love the Lord Thy God with all thy heart.*[1] Thou dost command me to love Thee, and to love Thee with all my heart. But if Thou didst not command me, O Jesus! how could I live without loving Thee, after so many proofs of Thy love? Yes, I love Thee, my supreme good; I love Thee with all my heart. I love Thee because Thou dost command me to love Thee. I love Thee because Thou art worthy of

[1] *Matt.* xxii. 37.

infinite love. I love Thee, and desire nothing else but to love Thee, and nothing else do I fear except being separated from Thee, and living without Thy love. Ah, my crucified love, permit not that I ever leave off loving Thee. Ever call to my remembrance the death that Thou hast undergone for me. Remind me of the endearments that Thou hast used towards me, and may the remembrance of them incite me more and more to love Thee, and to spend myself for Thee, who hast spent Thyself as a victim of love on the cross for me.

## XXXI.

*Qui etiam proprio Filio suo non pepercit, seal pro nobis omnibus tradidit il-ium quotnodo non etiam cum illo omnia nobis donavit?*

"He that spared not His only Son, but delivered Him up for us all, how hath He not also . . . given us all things? —*Rom.* viii. 32.

What flames of love ought not these words enkindle in our hearts: *Delivered Him up for us all!*[1] Divine justice, offended by our sins, must be satisfied; what, therefore, does God do? To pardon us, he wills that his Son should be condemned to death, and should himself pay the penalty due from us: *He spared not His only Son.*[2] O God! if the eternal Father were capable of suffering, what grief would he not have experienced in condemning to death, for the sins of his servants, his well-beloved and innocent Son! Let us imagine that we see the eternal Father, with Jesus dead in his arms, and saying, *For the*

[1] *Rom.* viii. 32.

[2] *Rom.* viii. 32.

*wickedness of My people have I struck Him.*[1] Rightly did St. Francis of Paula exclaim, in ecstasy of love, when meditating on the death of Jesus Christ, "O love! O love! O love!" On the other hand, with what confidence should not the following words inspire us: *How hath He not also, with Him, given us all things?*[2] And how, my God, should I fear that Thou shouldst not give me pardon, perseverance, Thy love, Thy Paradise, and all the graces that I can hope for, now that Thou hast given me that which is most dear to Thee, even Thine own Son? I know what I must do to obtain every good from Thee,—I must ask for it for the love of Jesus Christ; of this Jesus Christ himself assures me: *Amen, amen, say to you, if you ask the Father anything in My name, He will give it you.*[3]

My supreme and eternal God, I have hitherto despised Thy majesty and goodness; now I love Thee above all things; and because I love Thee, I repent with all my heart of having offended Thee, and would rather accept any chastisement than evermore offend Thee. Pardon me, and grant me those graces which I now ask of Thee, confiding in the promise of Jesus Christ. In the name of Jesus Christ I beseech Thee to give me holy perseverance to death, give me a pure and perfect love towards Thee, give me an entire conformity to Thy holy will, give me finally Paradise. I ask for all, and hope for all, from Thee through the merits of Jesus Christ. I deserve nothing; I am worthy of punishment, not of graces, but

[1] *Isa.* liii. 8.
[2] *Rom.* viii. 32.
[3] *John*, xvi. 23.

Thou dost deny nothing to those who pray to Thee for the love of Jesus Christ. Ah, my good God, I see that Thou dost wish me to be all Thine; I also wish to be Thine, and will not fear that my sins should prevent me from being all Thine, Jesus Christ has already satisfied for them, and Thou, besides, art ready, for the love of Jesus Christ, to give me all that I desire. This is my desire and my request; my God, hear me! I wish to love Thee, to love Thee exceedingly; and to be altogether Thine. Most holy Mary, help me.

## XXXII.

*Nos autem prœdicamus Christum crucifixum, Judœis quidem scandalum, Gentibus autem stultitiam.*

"But we preach Christ crucified, unto the Jews indeed a stumbling-block, and unto the Gentiles foolishness."—1 *Cor.* i. 23.

St. Paul assures us that the Gentiles, hearing it preached that the Son of God had been crucified for the salvation of mankind, reckoned it folly: *But unto the Gentiles foolishness;*[1] as if they said, Who can believe such folly, that a God should have willed to die for the love of his creatures! "It seems a foolish thing," says St. Gregory, "that a God should wish to die for the salvation of man." St. Mary Magdalen of Pazzi, also rapt in love, exclaims in an ecstasy, Do you not know, my sisters, that my Jesus is nothing but love? rather he is mad with love. I say that Thou art mad with love, my Jesus, and I will always say so.

My beloved Redeemer, oh that I could possess the hearts of all men, and with them love Thee as Thou

---

[1] 1 *Cor.* i. 23.

deservest to be loved! O God of love, why, after Thou hast shed all Thy blood in this world and given Thy life for the love of mankind, why, I say, are there so few men who burn with Thy love? For this end didst Thou come, namely, to kindle in our hearts the fire of Thy love, and Thou desirest nothing but to see it enkindled. *I am come to cast fire on the earth, and what will I but that it be kindled?* [1] I pray, then, with the Holy Church, in my name and in the name of every one living, kindle in them the fire of Thy love; enkindle them, enkindle them, enkindle them! My God, Thou art all goodness, all love, all infinite sweetness, boundless in love; make Thy self known to all, make Thyself loved. I am not ashamed of praying thus to Thee, although up to this time I have been more guilty than others in despising Thy love, because now, enlightened by Thy grace, and wounded by the many arrows of love Thou hast shot forth from Thy burning and loving heart into my soul, I am determined no longer to be ungrateful to Thee as I have hitherto been; but I will love Thee with all my strength, I desire to burn with Thy love, and this Thou hast to grant me. I look not for sensible consolations in loving Thee; I do not deserve them, neither do I ask for them; it is enough for me to love Thee. I love Thee, my sovereign good; I love Thee, my God and my all.

[1] *Luke*, xii. 49.

## XXXIII.

*Posuit Domimus in eo iniquitatem omnium nostrum. . . , et voluit conterere eum.*

"The Lord hath laid on Him the iniquity of us all. . . . And the Lord hath pleased to bruise Him."—*Isa.* liii. 6, 10.

Behold the extent of divine love towards man! The eternal Father loads the shoulders of his Son with our sins; *And He was pleased to bruise Him.* He willed that his own son should suffer with the utmost rigor all the punishment due to us, making him die on an ignominious cross overwhelmed with torments. The apostle is just, then, when speaking of this love, to call it too much love to ordain that we should receive life through the death of his beloved Son. *For His exceeding charity wherewith He loved us, even when we were dead in sins, hath quickened us together in Christ.*[1]

Thou hast, then, my God, loved me too much, and I have been too ungrateful in offending Thee and turning my back upon Thee. Ah, eternal Father, look upon Thine only-begotten, mangled and dead upon that cross for me, and for the love of him pardon me and draw my heart wholly to Thyself to love Thee. *A contrite and humble heart, O God, thou wilt not despise.*[2] For the love of Jesus Christ who died for our sins, Thou canst not despise a soul that humbles itself and repents. I know myself to be deserving of a thousand hells, but I repent with my whole heart for having offended Thee, the supreme Good. Reject me

---

[1] *Eph.* ii. 5.

[2] *Ps.* l. 19.

not, but have pity on me. But I am not content with a simple pardon; I desire that Thou shouldst give me a great love towards Thee, that I may compensate for all the offences that I have committed against Thee. I love Thee, infinite Goodness, I love Thee, O God of love. It is but little if I should die and annihilate myself for Thy sake. I desire to know how to love Thee as Thou deservest. But Thou knowest I can do nothing; do Thou make me grateful for the immense love that Thou hast had for me. I beg this of Thee for the love of Jesus, Thy Son. Grant that I may overcome everything in this life to please Thee, and that in death I may expire entirely united to Thy will, and so come to love Thee face to face with a perfect and eternal love in Paradise.

## XXXIV.

*Ego sum Pastor bonus. Bonus Pastor animam suam dat pro ovibus suis.*

"I am the Good Shepherd. The good shepherd giveth his life for his sheep."—*John*, x. ii.

My Jesus, what dost Thou say? What shepherd would ever give his life for his sheep? Thou alone, because Thou art a God of infinite love, canst say, *And I lay down My life for My sheep.*[1] Thou alone hast been able to show to the world this excess of love, that being our God and our supreme Lord, Thou hast yet willed to die for us. It was of this excess of love that Moses and Elias spoke on Mount Tabor: *They spoke of his decease that he should accomplish in Jerusalem.*[2] Hence St. John exhorts us to love a

[1] *John*, x. 15.

[2] *Luke*, ix. 31.

God who was the first to love us: *Let us therefore love God because God first hath loved us.*[1] As if he said, If we will not love this God for his infinite goodness, let us love him at least for the love that he has borne us in suffering willingly the pains that were due to us.

Remember, then, my Jesus, that I am one of those sheep for whom Thou hast given Thy life. Ah, cast on me one of those looks of pity with which Thou didst regard me once when Thou wast dying on the cross for me; look on me, change me, and save me. Thou hast called Thyself the loving Shepherd who, finding the lost sheep, takes it with joy and carries it on his shoulders, and then calls his friends to rejoice with him: *Rejoice with me, for I have found the sheep that was lost.*[2] Behold, I am the lost sheep; seek me and find me: *I have gone astray like a sheep that is lost; seek Thy servant.*[3] If through my fault Thou hast not yet found me, take me now and unite me and bind me to Thee, that Thou mayest not lose me again. The bond must be that of Thy love; if Thou dost not bind me with this sweet chain Thou wilt again lose me. Ah, it is not Thou who hast been wanting in binding me by holy love; but I, an ungrateful wretch, who have continually fled from Thee. But now I pray Thee, by that infinite mercy which caused Thee to come down to the earth to find me. Ah, bind me; but bind me with a double chain of love, that Thou mayest not lose me again, and that I may no more lose

---

[1] 1 *John*, iv. 19.

[2] *Luke*, xv. 6.

[3] *Ps.* cxviii. 176.

Thee. I renounce all the goods and pleasures of the world, and offer myself to suffer every pain, every death, provided that I live and die always united to Thee. I love Thee, my sweet Jesus; I love Thee, my good Shepherd, who hast died for Thy lost sheep; but know that this sheep now loves Thee more than himself, and desires nothing but to love Thee and to be consumed by Thy love. Have pity on him, then, and permit him never again to be separated from Thee.

## XXXV.

*Ego pono animam meam. . . . Nemo tollit eam a me, sed ego pono eam a meipso.*

"I lay down My life. . . . No one taketh it away from Me; but I lay it down of Myself."—*John,* x. 17, 18.

Behold, then, the Word Incarnate, urged alone by the love that he preserves towards us, accepts the death of the cross to give to man the life that he had lost. Behold, says St. Thomas, a God does for man more than he could have done if man had been (so to speak) his God, and as if God could never have been happy without man. "As if," these are the words of the saint, "man had been God's god, as if God could not be happy without him." We sinned, and by sinning merited eternal punishment; and what does Jesus do? He takes upon himself the obligation of satisfaction, and he pays for us by his sufferings and his death: *Surely he hath borne our infirmities and carried our sorrows?* [1]

Ah, my Jesus, since I have been the cause of all the bitterness and anguish that Thou didst suffer

[1] *Isa.* liii. 4.

while living on this earth, I pray Thee make me share the grief that Thou didst feel for my sins, and give me confidence in Thy Passion. What would have become of me, my Lord, if Thou hadst not deigned to satisfy for me? O infinite Majesty, I repent with my whole heart for having outraged Thee; but I hope for pity from Thee, who art infinite Goodness. Arise, O Saviour of the world, and apply to my soul the fruit of Thy death, and from an ungrateful rebel make me become such a true son as to love Thee alone, and to fear nothing but to displease Thee. May that same love which made Thee die on the cross for me destroy in me all earthly affections. My Jesus, take my whole body to Thyself in such a way that it may only serve to obey Thee; take my heart, that it may desire nothing but Thy pleasure; take my whole will, that it may wish for nothing but what is according to Thy will. I embrace Thee and press Thee to my heart, my Redeemer. Ah, do not disdain to unite Thyself to me. I love Thee, O God of love. I love Thee, my only good. How could I have the heart to leave Thee again, now that Thou hast taught me how much Thou hast loved me, and how many mercies Thou hast shown me, changing the punishments that were due to me into graces and caresses? O holy Virgin, obtain for me the grace of being grateful to thy Son.

## XXXVI.

*Delens quod adversus nos erat chirographum decreti, quod erat contrarium nobis, et ipsum tulit de medio, affigens illud cruci.*

"Blotting out the handwriting of the decree that was against us, which was contrary to us. And he hath taken the same out of the way, fastening it to the cross."—*Coloss.* ii. 14.

The sentence was already recorded against us that was to condemn us to eternal death, as rebels of the offended Majesty of God. And what has Jesus Christ done? With his blood he has cancelled the writing of the condemnation, and, to deliver us from all fear, he has fastened it to his own cross, on which he died to satisfy for us to the divine justice. My soul, behold the obligation that thou art under to thy Redeemer; and hear how the Holy Spirit now reminds thee: *Forget not the kindness of thy surety.*[1] Forget not the kindness of thy surety, who, taking upon himself thy debts, has paid them for thee; and behold, the pledge of the payment has been already fixed to the cross. When, therefore thou dost remember thy sins, look upon the cross, and have confidence; look on that sacred wood stained with the blood of the Lamb of God sacrificed for thy love, and hope in and love a God who has loved thee so much.

Yes, my Jesus, I hope everything from Thy infinite goodness. It is property of Thy divine nature to render good for evil to those who repent of their sins, are sorry for having committed them, and who love Thee.

---

[1] *Ecclus.* xxix. 20.

Yes, I am sorry above all things, my beloved Redeemer, for having so much despised Thy goodness, and, wounded by Thy love, I love Thee, and I ardently desire to please Thee in everything that is Thy will. Alas! when I was in sin, I was the servant of the devil, and he was my master. Now that I hope to remain in Thy grace, Thou alone, my Jesus, art the only Lord of my heart, and my only Love. Take possession of me, then; keep me always, possess me entirely; for Thine only do I desire to be. No, nevermore will I forget the pains that Thou hast suffered for me; so shall I be more and more inflamed, and increase in Thy love. I love Thee, my most dear Redeemer; I love Thee, O Word Incarnate; my treasure, my all, I love Thee, I love Thee.

## XXXVII.

*Si quis peccaverit, advocatum habemus apud Patrem Jesum Christum justum, et ipse est propitiatio pro peccatis nostris.*

"But if any man sin, we have an Advocate with the Father, Jesus Christ the Just, and he is the propitiation for our sins."—1 *John*, ii. i.

Oh, what great confidence do these words give to penitent sinners! Jesus Christ is in heaven, advocating their cause, and he is certain to obtain pardon for them. The devil, when a sinner has escaped from his chains, tempts him to be diffident of obtaining pardon. But St. Paul encourages him, saying, *Who is He that shall condemn? Jesus Christ that died, . . . who also maketh intercession for us.*[1] The Apostle means to say, If we detest the sins that we have committed, why do we fear? Who is he who will condemn us? It

[1] *Rom.* viii. 34.

is Jesus Christ, the same who died, that we might not be condemned, and who is now in heaven, where he is advocating our cause. He goes on to say, *Who then shall separate us from the love of Christ?* [1] As if he would say, But after we have been pardoned with so much love by Jesus Christ, and have been received into his grace, who could have the heart to turn his back upon him, and separate himself from his love?

No, my Jesus, I no longer rely upon myself so as to live separated from Thee and deprived of Thy love. I weep over the unhappy days when lived without Thy grace. Now I hope that Thou hast pardoned me I love Thee, and Thou lovest me. But Thou dost love with a boundless love, and I love Thee so little; give me more love. Infinite Goodness, I repent above all things for having hitherto so ill-treated Thee; now I love Thee above all things, I love Thee more than myself; and I take more delight, my God, in knowing that Thou art infinitely blessed than in my own happiness, because I love Thee better being, as Thou art, worthy of infinite love than myself, who deserve nothing but hell. My Jesus, I wish for nothing from Thee, but Thyself.

## XXXVIII.

*Venite ad me omnes, qui laboratis et onerati estis, et ego reficiam vos.*

"Come to Me, all you that labor, and are burdened, and I will refresh you."—*Matt.* xi. 28.

Let us listen to Jesus Christ, who from the cross to which he is nailed, and from the altar where he dwells under the sacramental species, calls us poor

[1] *Rom.* viii. 35.

afflicted sinners to console us and enrich us with his graces. Oh, what two great mysteries of hope and love to us are the Passion of Jesus Christ and the Sacrament of the Eucharist! mysteries which, if faith did not make us certain of them, would be incredible. That God should deign to shed even the very last drop of his blood! (for this is the signification of *effundetur*). *This is My Blood, . . . which shall be shed for many.*[1] And why? To atone for our sins. But then to will to give his own body as food for our souls, that body which had already been sacrificed on the cross for our salvation! These sublime mysteries must surely soften the hardest hearts, and raise up the most desperate sinners. Finally, the Apostle says that in Jesus Christ we are enriched with every good, so that no grace is wanting to us: *In all things you are made rich in Him. . . . So that nothing is wanting to you in any grace.*[2] It is enough that we invoke this God for him to have mercy on us; and he will abound in grace to all who pray to him, as the same Apostle as sures us: *Rich unto all who call upon Him.*[3]

If, then, my Saviour, I have reason to despair of pardon for the offences and treacheries that I have been guilty of towards Thee, I have still greater reason to trust in Thy goodness. My Father, I have forsaken Thee, like an ungrateful son; but I now return to Thy feet, full of sorrow and covered with confusion for the many mercies that Thou hast shown me; and I say with shame, *Father, I am not*

---

[1] *Matt.* xxvi. 28.

[2] 1 *Cor.* i. 5.

[3] *Rom.* x. 12.

*worthy to be called Thy son.*[1] Thou hast said that there is rejoicing in heaven when a sinner is converted: *There shall be joy in heaven upon one sinner that doth penance.*[2] Behold, I leave all and turn to Thee, my crucified Father; I repent with my whole heart for having treated Thee with such contempt as to turn my back upon Thee. Receive me again to Thy grace, and inflame with Thy holy love, so that I may never leave Thee again. Thou hast said, *I am come that they may have life, and may have it more abundantly.*[3] Wherefore I hope to receive from Thee, not only Thy grace as I enjoyed it before I offended Thee, but a grace more abundant, which shall make me become all on fire with Thy love. Oh that I could love Thee, my God, as Thou dost deserve to be loved! I love Thee above all things. I love Thee more than myself. I love Thee with all my heart; and I aspire after heaven, where I shall love Thee for all eternity. *What is there to me in heaven, and besides Thee what have I desired on earth? O God, God of my heart and my portion forever.*[4] Ah, God of my heart, take and keep possession of all my heart, and drive from it every affection that does not belong to Thee. Thou art my only treasure, my only love. I wish for Thee alone, and nothing more. O Mary, my hope, by thy prayers draw me all to God.

---

[1] *Luke*, xv. 21.
[2] *Luke*, xv. 7.
[3] *John*, x. 10.
[4] *Ps.* lxxii. 25.

COR
JESU

*Charitas enim Christi urget nos.*

**2 Corinthians v. 14.**

* 9 7 9 8 9 8 9 1 6 6 1 8 3 *

20250105180355